CW01501176

Tigers at Dunkirk

Tigers at Dunkirk

The Leicestershire Regiment and the Fall of France

Matthew Richardson

Pen & Sword
MILITARY

First published in Great Britain in 2010 by
PEN & SWORD MILITARY
an imprint of
Pen & Sword Books Ltd
47 Church Street
Barnsley
South Yorkshire
S70 2AS

© Matthew Richardson 2010

ISBN 978–1–84884–210–6

A CIP catalogue record for this book is available from the British Library.

Typeset in Ehrhardt by Concept, Huddersfield, West Yorkshire
Printed and bound in England by CPI UK

Pen & Sword Books Ltd incorporates the Imprints of Pen & Sword Aviation, Pen & Sword Maritime, Pen & Sword Military, Wharncliffe Local History, Pen & Sword Select, Pen & Sword Military Classics, Leo Cooper, Remember When, Seaforth Publishing and Frontline Publishing

For a complete list of Pen & Sword titles please contact
Pen & Sword Books Limited
47 Church Street, Barnsley, South Yorkshire, S70 2AS, England
E-mail: enquiries@pen-and-sword.co.uk
Website: www.pen-and-sword.co.uk

Contents

For Natalia

List of Maps

List of Plates

Private J.L. 'Moe' Harper.

Platoon Sergeant Major T.F. Simpson.

The road bridge over the Deule Canal at Pont a Vendin.

Section 2

German troops make an assault crossing of a canal using rubber dinghies, May 1940.

French Senegalese POWs being marched to the rear.

Corporal Andrew Quigley.

Private Don French.

The triage slip given to Don French in hospital.

Private Joseph Gamble.

Private Phil Haywood.

Private Freddie Diaper.

Private Dick Cobley.

Lieutenant Richard Everard.

Private Harold Simons.

The canal at Coudekerque.

Private Harry Crane.

The Isle of Man Steam Packet vessel *Mona's Isle*.

Sergeant Ian C. Noble.

Private Alf Nichols.

SS *Royal Eagle*.

The Channel Islands ferry *St Helier*.

Private Gordon Spring.

Lance Corporal Sid Garner.

Private Arthur Knight.

Lance Corporal Ron Riches and his bride.

Sergeant John Dwyer.

Lance Corporal Ronald 'Clem' Webster.

Private Victor Clough.

Regimental Quartermaster Sergeant Joe French.

Foreword

In September 1939 the British Expeditionary Force (BEF) was sent to France to fight against the German Army, which was well armed with infantry and panzer divisions. The British soldiers were poorly equipped and stood no chance against the Germans. My battalion, the 2nd/5th Leicestershire Regiment of 139th Brigade in the 46th North Midland Infantry Division, was shipped out in April 1940. Our arms and transport were quite inadequate for the job we were expected to do – we infantrymen had First World War Lee-Enfield bolt-action rifles.

On 10 May 1940 the Germans invaded Holland, Belgium and France. This ended the Phoney War, and our division was sent up to Belgium to the front line. At no time did we fight as a division, it was always by brigades. Land supply routes had been mainly destroyed by the German air force, so supplies never got to forward units. Roads were blocked with refugees with all their worldly goods, and a German breakthrough meant we were ordered to pull back. At Carvin we were bombed by Stukas, and received orders from above to head for Dunkirk.

After some days on the road, in the distance we saw great columns of black smoke, and we were told to head towards it. We were picking up anything edible out of the fields as we had had no food for some time. At Dunkirk we were directed to La Panne beaches. What a sight met our eyes, lines and lines of troops in queues, all just waiting for boats to come in and to be picked up. Troops were wading out up to their armpits and being dragged into small boats. My small group eventually made it to the front of our queue and we were loaded on to a boat.

This had been the biggest retreat and defeat ever suffered by the British Army, but what could we do without the required equipment? We took a real hammering. It could have been catastrophic for our country if it was not for the brilliance, determination and courage of our great Royal Navy, and the owners of the little ships, who did a fantastic job. The number of troops safely brought home was 338,220. An amazing job, well carried out. When I was called up just after war was declared, I had no idea what I would be facing for the next six-and-a-half years. To do what our country and its allies did to Hitler, after such a start, is a fantastic achievement.

It is now seventy years since Dunkirk and survivors are fast fading away. Those of us that are left can still remember the hardships we suffered, but also what we accomplished. To the people of Leicestershire, the present-day generation and to future generations, I hope you will buy, read and digest this book. It is after all about your regiment, the Royal Leicestershires. The Tigers fought in every great battle worldwide, beating the Japanese into the bargain.

I would like to thank the author of this book, Mr Matthew Richardson, for his very hard work in collecting information and having the book ready for the seventieth anniversary. I thank him as well for his interest in my battalion and regiment, and for ensuring that my comrades who fell are not forgotten – a wonderful job Matthew. Thanks must also go to Mrs Richardson, for all the cups of tea she must have made for him along the way!

Ex-Corporal J.L. 'Moe' Harper 4860940
A, B, and HQ coys, 2nd/5th battalion the
Royal Leicestershire Regiment – a survivor

Introduction and Acknowledgements

This book chronicles the actions of the 2nd/5th battalion of the Leicestershire Regiment in 1940 – its background, the way it was raised, the men who made it and its part in the campaign in France in the summer of that year which culminated in the evacuation of the British Army from Dunkirk. The title of the book of course belies the whole story. Some of the men featured herein will never actually have taken part in the evacuation, nor even set foot in the town of Dunkirk. Some were killed or taken prisoner before the battalion began its winding and weary retreat to the French coast, but they are as much a part of the story of this campaign as those who came back from it. The book goes on to examine the experiences in captivity of those members of the battalion who were made POWs in 1940.

The publication of the book marks the conclusion of a ten-year journey upon which I have found myself. At a personal level it represents the achievement of a long-held ambition to complete the Leicestershire Regiment trilogy which I began in 1998 (the other books being *The Tigers* and *Fighting Tigers*) and although it is the last of the three, in many ways it was there in the background right from the start. I have probably since childhood had an interest in the battles of 1940 and the Dunkirk evacuation. This short chapter of the Second World War, which began on 10 May 1940 and lasted less than a month, contains as much drama as some other far longer campaigns.

In particular I felt that the participation of the Leicestershire Regiment in this episode deserved to be explored more fully. When I embarked upon this project there were only two published works that dealt with the 2nd/5th Leicesters in France in 1940 – one was Brigadier W.E. Underhill's official history of the regiment, the other was my own *Fighting Tigers*. Neither really did it justice. As far as I was aware, nothing else had appeared in print on the subject. There were certainly no published memoirs as such – soldiers usually do not like to dwell on defeats and perhaps veterans of the campaign felt it was best left forgotten. Likewise, in recent years two major books have appeared about the 1940 French campaign, both by high-profile and well-respected authors. One mentions the 2nd/5th Leicesters in passing, the other fails to mention the battalion at all.

Yet for me there were a lot of unanswered questions. Whilst the battalion had undoubtedly been completely overpowered by the Germans and forced into a humiliating retreat, I felt that more needed to be said about how, where and why this had happened. There were also many individual stories of bravery and of personal sacrifice which I felt needed to be told, both on the part of the men who made it back and of those who did not.

It was hearing a family friend, Don French, talk about his experiences as a prisoner of war which first started me thinking about this project. A couple of years later I met Victor Clough at a regimental reunion. His personal story of commandeering a boat to row to England fascinated me, yet it had never been documented. I'm pleased to say that Victor's story now forms part of this book. Sadly many of the other men who started this journey with me, such as Don French, are no longer with us to see its conclusion. I remember vividly sitting in Don's kitchen while he described POW life, and I hope that he and the other veterans who contributed to this book would have been proud of what we have jointly achieved.

I would like to mention a number of other people who have assisted in this project, some of them are the 'usual suspects', others were previously strangers but whose acquaintance I am delighted to have made as a result of this project: Mr and Mrs Arlott, Jim Blair, Alan Briggs, Mrs L. Chaplin, Terry Dwyer, Joan Haywood, Marjorie Moore, Harold Simons, Pat England, John Chambers, David Botibol, Mrs M. Garner, Bobby Riches, Jean Richardson, Ken Paterson, Carole Wheat, Joe French, Major A.E.R. Ross, Irene Malin, Sue Jordan, Richard Vincent and Adrian Woolley. Colonel Anthony Swallow OBE, as in the past, has offered me much encouragement. I greatly value his personal support and that of the Royal Tigers Association. Greg Drozdz in Hinckley has been of tremendous help, as he has with my previous projects. J.L. 'Moe' Harper patiently answered my many questions, and similarly Major Peter Moore MC allowed me to question him at great length and also offered valuable advice. Andrew Quigley provided me with photos and information relating to his late father. Robin Jenkins at the Record Office for Leicestershire, Leicester and Rutland has, as so many times previously, been a great help in locating archival treasures. I would also like to thank Margaret Bonney for permission to reproduce material held by the record office. Philip French at Leicester Museums was also helpful, as was Kevin Asplin who undertook a great deal of research at the National Archives on my behalf – I thank him warmly. Maurice Jennings, a former POW of the 2nd/5th battalion, kindly answered my numerous questions. Captain Kerry Noble provided a great deal of information about his father and allowed me to use material that he had placed on the BBC 'People's War' website. Mel Gould, whom I have known for a number of years, also kept his ear to the ground for information for me and provided valuable leads and sources.

I would like to pay particular tribute to Gordon Spring, of Hinckley. Gordon very generously allowed me to quote from his book *Gordon the Tiger*, which covers not just his experiences at Dunkirk but also his later war service. The book is available from Voluntary Action Hinckley & Bosworth, on Waterloo Road, Hinckley and costs £5. Proceeds go to the Royal British Legion Poppy Appeal. Likewise, Horace 'Jim' Greasley kindly allowed me to use material from his book *Do The Birds Still Sing In Hell?*, published by Libros International. Ken Scott, who ghost wrote the book with Horace, was also incredibly forthcoming with his time and help. I thank them both.

Richard Everard very kindly permitted me to quote from his father's unpublished memoir *A Soldier's Tale*. This was of immeasurable help to me and I thank him and other members of the Everard family. Peter Gee provided much information about his father Captain Geoff Gee and I was thus able to learn a great deal about his lifelong friendship with Lieutenant Everard. Captain Nicholas Oliver and his family allowed me to quote from the report prepared by Lieutenant Colonel Kenneth Ruddle concerning the events covered by this book, for which I am most grateful.

Fellow author Michael Kendrick provided photographs and information. Michael will be familiar to many. He has produced a series of lavishly illustrated books covering the Leicestershire Regiment and Leicestershire people in both world wars. Michael has always been more than willing to share his material and I salute him for his generosity of spirit.

Frank and Joan Shaw, authors of *We Remember Dunkirk*, proved impossible to locate despite my best efforts to track them down. I am nonetheless grateful to them for their foresight in preserving memories of Dunkirk in 1990, at a time when there were still a good number of survivors around and those memories were still very fresh. Extracts from that book used herein are duly credited to Frank and Joan.

Jim and Philip Monk very kindly allowed me access to their late father Bob's photographs, and this has greatly enhanced the book. I'm enormously grateful to them. Jim and Philip's sister Barbara Mclish helped me by filling in a lot of detail about her father. Likewise, Pat English offered me a great deal of information about her father and his experiences as a POW.

Andrew Johnson, Allison Fox and Sara Simpson read my typescript and offered many suggestions and improvements, for which I am most grateful. I would like to thank Rupert Harding and Pen & Sword Limited for once again taking my ideas on board and producing a fantastic book. I'd also like to thank my family. Mum, Dad and Natalia, thanks for all your encouragement. Lucie and Katie, I hope that one day you will enjoy reading this and realise why sometimes I was too busy to play football with you.

Lastly, I am tremendously honoured that 'Moe' Harper has agreed to write the foreword to the book. In most books, the foreword is written by an esteemed dignitary or similar worthy person, but in this case I regard it as a great seal of approval to have the foreword written by an ordinary soldier – someone who was actually present at the events that the book describes. I'm sure Mr Harper will not mind me describing him as 'ordinary', even though he is not. He is one of life's gentlemen, and at 90 years of age he remains impressively sharp. Our paths first crossed in 2000, when I was working on *Fighting Tigers*, with which he was also a great help. I myself feel deeply humbled by the debt that my generation owes to his. This book is really about paying tribute to those brave men of 1940 before it is too late, and in some small way I hope that it goes towards acknowledging the debt that we in Britain owe to men like him and the sacrifices that others of his generation made to keep us free. I make no apology for the fact that I borrowed this phrase from a car bumper sticker, but if you can read this, thank a teacher. If you can read it in English, thank a soldier.

The author would be pleased to hear from anyone with a family connection to the Leicestershire Regiment, from any era, and can be contacted via the publishers or through the website www.green-tiger.co.uk.

Matthew Richardson
Isle of Man, January 2010

Chapter 1

Birth of a Battalion

The 1930s were unsettled times in Europe. Adolf Hitler's National Socialist (Nazi) Party had come to power in Germany in 1933, and was bent on two major objectives. The first was the restoration of German pride and honour following what many in that country perceived as the humiliation of defeat in the First World War. The second objective, closely linked to the first, was the overturning of the punitive peace terms imposed upon Germany at the Treaty of Versailles in 1919. Hitler, intent on making Germany a power to be reckoned with once again, began to re-arm. At the same time, the major western powers, France and Great Britain, seemed too wrapped up in their own domestic problems to offer much in the way of opposition to Hitler's demands for the return of territories lost in 1919 to Poland and Czechoslovakia. The battalion that was to become known as the 2nd/5th Leicestershire was born out of the Munich Crisis of 1938, when Hitler was temporarily bought off by the western leaders. He had been handed a large chunk of Czechoslovakia, but in spite of Prime Minister Neville Chamberlain's assurances of 'peace in our time', by this stage it had become apparent to all but the most idealistic that ultimately there would be no appeasing Adolf Hitler. The only question was when, not if, there would be a new war with Germany.

Belatedly Britain began to re-arm after the parsimonious years of the 1930s. One measure that was quickly effected (on paper at least) was a doubling of the size of the Territorial Army. Britain's Territorials trace their roots back to the rifle volunteer battalions of the nineteenth century. By the time of the First World War, the Territorial Force had become an important auxiliary corps, made up of part-time volunteers, which supported the Regular Army in time of war. Indeed, the Territorial Force had fought so well in the First World War that in the 1920s HM King George V had bestowed upon it the new title of Territorial Army (TA), an army being more prestigious than a mere force. One of the great strengths of the TA was its local roots. All of the recruits were drawn from a small geographical area and the officers were usually members of the local gentry or wealthy local businessmen. These local roots did much to foster *esprit de corps* within the TA.

The new Territorial battalions were to be raised using the same method that had been employed during the First World War. Certain battalions were selected to be split, and form a new 1st and 2nd battalion. Thus the 5th battalion of the Leicestershire Regiment (which, it can be said without exaggeration, was one of the finest Territorial battalions in the country at that time) was split into a 1st/5th which largely drew its recruits from the wider county and a 2nd/5th which was largely based on Leicester and its outskirts. C Company of the old battalion, based at Hinckley, was to provide the nucleus of trained men and was transferred *en bloc* together with its officers, including Captain Mike Moore, to become D Company of the new battalion. Moore was one of the most popular Territorial officers in the regiment. Regarded as likeable and fun to be with by his fellow officers, he had been commissioned into the 5th battalion in 1934 aged 18, after leaving Eastbourne College. In civil life, Mike worked for the family firm of Moore Eady knitwear, located on Stockwell Head in Hinckley.

For the first few months at least, enlistment in this new formation was to be on a purely voluntary basis and a nationwide appeal was made for volunteers to fill the ranks of the TA. One of the first to join was Dick Vincent of Leicester who, spurred on by a sense of duty to his country, went along with two pals to the Magazine on Leicester's Oxford Street in order to enlist. There are many parallels between the raising of this new battalion (which despite being administered by the county Territorial Association was in essence a war service only formation) and the raising of the Kitchener's Army battalions of the Leicestershire Regiment in the First World War. In both cases, battalions were raised under conditions of extreme difficulty. Both faced shortages of equipment. Both had problems of unsatisfactory accommodation. Both had a very limited timescale of around six to eight months in which to turn raw recruits into something approaching fighting soldiers (which in peacetime took around two years) and in both cases officers struggled hard to maintain the morale and initial enthusiasm of their recruits when faced with these trying circumstances.

Command of the new battalion fell to Major Guy German, who had been the senior Major of the old 5th battalion. The German family had strong links with the Leicestershire Regiment going back at least a generation. His father, Lieutenant Colonel George German, had in fact commanded a previous 2nd/5th battalion during the First World War. Just too young to have served in that war, Guy German had been commissioned into the 5th battalion in 1921. By the outbreak of the Second World War he had seen the battalion evolve from one in which every officer rode a charger and the main topic in the officers' mess was hunting, to one at the highest state of efficiency for a Territorial battalion in the 1930s. Guy German was destined to be captured, not in France but in Norway, and would spend the rest of the war as a prisoner. For some of this time he was Senior British Officer (SBO) in Oflag IVC, the infamous Colditz Castle, where the diarist J. Ellison Platt wrote of him: 'No one is under any misapprehension as to why Guy German is being removed. He is as much a soldier in the field while in prison as before his capture. His almost ferocious loyalty to British escape interests has won commendation from all nationalities.'[1]

Gordon Spring of Hinckley had joined C Company just before the split. Back then there was still a certain amateur quality about the TA:

> At 14 years I left school and like many of my friends went into the hosiery factories, working on the fully fashioned machines at Fludes. Although I earned money I had to start from 6.00 in the morning until 8.00 at night.
>
> In early 1939 Mr Flude said that we should join the Territorial Army in Hinckley, which I had made up my mind to do some time before. I was used to sleeping three in a bed at home and yet what a change – sleeping on the Drill Hall floor by myself – I loved being a soldier. I got top marks for smartness ...
>
> Before we left Hinckley I used to parade in the car park and then at the Regent Cinema. My guard duties were in Brunel Road and one day my sister arrived with some supper from my mother. She said that Mother wanted me to come home now. I told her 'I'm in the ruddy army now!' I felt a bit like Private Pike in *Dad's Army*. I put my rifle down and started to eat my supper. The Sergeant Major came along and said, 'Is that your rifle Private Spring?' 'Yes Sir', I replied. He said, 'What if the enemy came now – how the bloody hell do you expect to defend the drill hall?' I was confined to barracks for three days.[2]

Britain, however, was sliding towards war and in April 1939 the Military Training Act was introduced. This halfway house was not quite conscription but required all men not in a reserved occupation to register for six months' military training. These were the so-called 'Militiamen'.

The 2nd/5th battalion's only annual camp was held at Holyhead, on Anglesey in North Wales that summer, 1939. Although reasonable progress could be made with individual training and field craft, what was less easy to work around were deficiencies in heavy equipment. As the country frantically tried to re-arm, call upon the newest equipment naturally went to the Regular

Army. The TA had to make do with at best outdated equipment, and that was if anything was obtainable at all. The battalion had no Bren Carriers, and no weapons heavier than .303 Lee-Enfield rifles. The only transport it could muster comprised civilian vans and lorries, and for troops to be transported in this fashion (which was later parodied in the television programme *Dad's Army* when the platoon are transported in Corporal Jones' butcher's shop van) can hardly have been good for morale.

Nevertheless, the August 1939 edition of the regimental newspaper the *Green Tiger* reported on the success of the camp, where both 1st/5th and 2nd/5th battalions had trained together. In reporting on the 2nd/5th battalion, however, it noted rather dryly that: 'We have a complete Band ready to serve, and indications are that it is going to be a very good one. It is however to be regretted that the Treasury do not appear eager to assist us in this direction and several others.'[3] It went on to note that when a newly formed unit camps with an older established one, there is bound to be some degree of envy in regard to the standard and quality of the equipment of the latter as opposed to the former. The report on the 2nd/5th however ended philosophically:

> It is these little points which are all too apt to be overlooked, but which really mean a great deal to any commander who is asked to raise a new unit. None the less, we are all of us mindful of the fact that 'the finest thing a man can have the opportunity of doing is to be asked to raise a new unit in His Majesty's Army', and we hope, and believe, we shall take fullest advantage of this opportunity.[4]

One of the best and brightest young officers of the 2nd/5th at the Holyhead camp was Second Lieutenant Harold Driver. The previous year, 1938, he had attended the annual camp at Thursley as a cadet officer with Uppingham School OTC. Whilst there he had been invited to have lunch with the officers of the 5th battalion Leicestershire Regiment. He made a good impression and was subsequently commissioned into the regiment. At Holyhead, aged only 19, he found himself commanding a company of the newly formed 2nd/5th battalion. Undaunted by the responsibility, he went about his duties in a quiet but efficient way. He quickly gained the respect of the often much older men under his command, not always an easy thing for a junior officer to do. He held much promise for the future and would undoubtedly have been a 'rising star' of the battalion. Sadly only two months later he was killed in a motor car accident. It was a loss the battalion could ill afford. A measure of the esteem in which he was held by his men may be judged by the fact that, despite having just finished a 24-hour stint of guard duty, the men of his company as a unit asked for permission to attend his funeral.

Upon return from the Holyhead camp, the battalion acquired new billets – the disused shoe factory of Messrs V. & A. Thompson on Eastern Boulevard, Leicester. The *Green Tiger* again rather dryly reported: 'We can, at the moment, remark with satisfaction that we will have a very fine view of the river from most of our windows which will no doubt sound very well to those readers of this journal who do not know the River Soar at that particular spot.'[5]

The shortfall in officers for the new battalion was made good by commissioning some of the more able sergeants from the old 5th battalion, including Sergeant Charlie Hughes and 20-year-old Sergeant Robert Sharp. Robert was the son of Mr W.M. Sharp, who owned a firm of builders on East Short Street in Leicester. An old Wyggestonian, Sharp was also a keen sportsman, playing football for Westleigh FC and cricket for Leicester Town CC. At the time of his enlistment he was studying building engineering. Charlie Hughes, meanwhile, came from Oadby, and worked for the Bass, Ratcliffe and Gretton Brewery. He had joined the TA as a private soldier in 1938, and was quickly promoted to sergeant. He transferred to the 2nd/5th battalion when it was formed, and reached the rank of Regimental Quartermaster Sergeant before applying successfully for a commission.

Somewhat older than Sharp and Hughes was Second Lieutenant Sidney Brown. He was born in Leicester on 17 July 1906 and was educated at the Stoneygate and Wyggeston Schools in Leicester, and Rossall School in Lancashire. On leaving school in 1924, he had joined his father, Thomas William Brown, in the family business of Rockleys Limited, Outdoor Advertising Contractors. In 1928 the company changed its name to Mills and Rockleys Ltd following the amalgamation of a number of midland companies, and is still responsible for many large advertising hoardings today under the name Mills and Allen. In the early 1930s Brown became interested in social improvement work in Leicester, in particular the work of boys' clubs in deprived areas. He took over the leadership of the Shaftesbury St George's Boys' Club in George Street, Leicester, and ran the club himself until the outbreak of war. At the same time he became interested in political work, through assisting with campaigning in the Melton constituency in 1931 and later in the East Leicester division.

In 1938 Sidney Brown was asked to stand as the Conservative candidate for the Aylestone ward and was subsequently elected a member of Leicester City

Council. His route into the 2nd/5th battalion was somewhat unusual. That same year, in order to boost recruitment he was photographed whilst signing on as a lowly private soldier in the ranks of the 5th battalion of Leicestershire Regiment, despite being a serving Tory councillor. The photograph subsequently appeared in Leicester newspapers as part of the countywide recruiting campaign for the TA. Brown did not long remain in the ranks, however. Shortly afterwards he was commissioned, and in 1939 he was transferred to the 2nd/5th battalion where he would ultimately command HQ Company. He was still serving as an elected member of the City Council when the battalion went to war.

On the morning of Sunday, 3 September 1939, Britain was stunned by the news crackling from thousands of wireless sets in living rooms across the country. Germany had not responded to Britain's ultimatum to withdraw her troops from Poland, which she had invaded two days previously. A state of war would thus exist between Britain and Germany, only twenty-one years after the previous devastating war between the two countries had drawn to a close.

Private Joseph Kynoch of Loughborough remembered how the escalating tensions in Europe in the run up to war had led to a general mobilisation of the TA, and how the actual news was received:

The war began for me and most of my comrades of 2/5 battalion the Leicestershire Regiment on Monday 28 August 1939, after our annual summer camp at Holyhead, North Wales. The buff envelope with the letters OHMS on it dropped through our letterbox at home. It ordered me briefly to report at the TA centre on Friday, September 1st, and it was on that very day that the German army crossed the border into Poland. We knew then that Britain would have to declare war on Germany along with France and this would be the beginning of the Second World War and the end of our personal freedom as we had known it and that from now on we would have no choice but to obey any orders which were given from above, starting with Lance Corporal.

I remember that sunny Sunday morning, September 3rd, when we marched through the centre of Leicester as a battalion, with bayonets fixed and watched by cheering crowds of people and with the Regimental band playing at the head of the column on the way to church. I felt very proud at that moment to be in the Leicesters.

At eleven o'clock, the service was interrupted by the Prime Minister's voice on the wireless in the church, telling us that the ultimatum which

Britain had given to Hitler to withdraw his troops from Poland by 11.00am otherwise a state of war would exist between Germany and Britain and France, had expired and no reply had been received, consequently we were now at war with Germany.[6]

No one this time was under any illusion as to what total war meant. This time there would be no half measures and no appealing to the nation for volunteers. In October 1939, compulsory full-time military service was introduced. Thus the 2nd/5th battalion was to consist of three categories of men: pre-war Territorial volunteers, Militiamen and wartime conscripts.

George Arlott of Kimberley Road, Leicester was one of the latter. He was working as a process engraver in the printing trade when in October 1939 he received a letter instructing him to report to Glen Parva barracks near Wigston, the depot of the Leicestershire Regiment. His chief memory of this period, other than target practice on the Kibworth rifle range, was endless square bashing under the watchful eye of a drill sergeant. At this point in time Arlott was not a member of any particular battalion, his nominal unit was simply the depot, but fate was about to play a hand in his future. He remembered: 'The company I was in – I had the flu – and while I was in hospital (I was that bad I was in hospital) the Company I was in got sent to Singapore – and got captured. So it was bad for me, but not as bad as it was for them.'[7]

Arlott subsequently found himself posted to the 2nd/5th battalion. His illness had narrowly prevented his joining the ill-fated 1st battalion, which after a dreadful battering during the Japanese invasion of Malaya was forced to surrender *en bloc* to the enemy in February 1942. Although Arlott himself was later to fall into German hands, his privations were as nothing compared to the suffering of those in Japanese captivity.

Horace Greasley was a barber by trade, and one of twin brothers from Ibstock. He had been working away from home in Torquay during the busy summer season in 1939, but had registered for conscription at his home address, 101 Pretoria Road, Ibstock. He received his call-up papers in the autumn of 1939 and returned home. Initially both he and his brother had been called up together but his brother being devoutly religious had applied for – and received – exemption from front-line service on the grounds of conscientious objection, and was posted to the Royal Army Medical Corps in a non-combatant role. Horace, meanwhile, had received instructions to report to a recruiting office in Leicester – he was to join the 2nd/5th Leicesters. The first night in billets on Eastern Boulevard his comrades christened him 'Jim', as it was felt that Horace was not sufficiently warlike, and it was by this name that he was to be known throughout the rest of his military service.

A fourth group of men was soon to join the battalion because shortages in NCOs were, to a large extent, addressed by utilising reservists who had served previously with the Regular Army. One such was Sergeant Fred Smith of West Bridgford, Nottingham who had first joined the Leicestershire Regiment as a 17-year-old in 1930. He had then been posted to the 1st battalion at Ambala in India. For Fred, Army life in India in the 1930s was much the same as it had been for generations of British soldiers in the preceding sixty or so years. Parades and training took place in the early part of the day, before the heat became too intense. In the middle part of the day, soldiers were confined to their Victorian barrack blocks where Indian children or old men pulled long ropes to swing the punkahs hanging from the ceiling. The sights and smells of the East must have made a deep impression on a young lad from West Bridgford, but after completing his seven years' colour service in 1937, Fred had returned home to Blighty. He was still on his five years of reserve service when in 1939 the war began, and he was recalled to the 2nd/5th battalion. This would have been a far cry from his previous military experiences on the dusty plains of India, and it is easy to imagine 'old sweats' like Smith regaling raw young conscripts with their stories of foreign service in exotic locations. These reservists were further augmented by NCOs recalled for the purpose from the 1st battalion, still in India, and the other regular battalion, the 2nd, which was based in Palestine. They joined the 2nd/5th in France before the fighting began.

The outbreak of war brought another change among the officers. Over in the sister 1st/5th battalion, the commanding officer, Lieutenant Colonel John Barrett VC (in civilian life a surgeon at Leicester Royal Infirmary), had been transferred to the Royal Army Medical Corps. The vacancy at the head of this battalion was filled by Major Guy German, next in order of seniority, and this in turn created a vacancy at the head of the 2nd/5th battalion. Major Kenneth Ruddle, a Rutland man, Deputy Lieutenant of that county and a member of the local brewing family responsible for 'Ruddle's County' and other well-known beers, was promoted to take charge of the battalion. Ruddle was another long-serving Territorial officer, who had been commissioned into the battalion in the early 1920s alongside Guy German. Ruddle's second in command was now to be Major Kenneth Symington, a member of another prominent local family with long-standing connections to the 5th battalion. The Symingtons were major employers in Market Harborough, both as food and garment manufacturers. Ken Symington's involvement with the old 5th battalion had begun when he was commissioned into the battalion in 1925. Early in his service career he took over command of the old D Company of the 5th battalion, based at Coalville. Despite the distance from his home, through hard work and commitment he had won the respect of the Coalville miners, who made up the bulk of the company. A typical example of one of these men would be Corporal Arthur Chambers, who would go on to become Company Sergeant Major of HQ Company. A hard-working coal-face miner at one of Coalville's pits, he had joined the Territorial Army at the town's drill hall in the early 1930s. It is important to remember that in those days the TA offered him and men like him both the chance to top up their pay and, just as importantly, a week's holiday at the annual camp, which was often held near the coast at places like Scarborough. Senior NCOs could even take their families along with them, an attractive perk in itself.

Second Lieutenant Jack Townsend, a trainee engineer with Jones & Shipman in Leicester who had been with the battalion since Holyhead, now became the Signals Officer. Some fresh young officers were also now commissioned directly into the battalion, including Second Lieutenant N.D. Stickland and Second Lieutenant Cliff Marriott. Richard Everard, who hailed from Woodhouse Eaves, was another new face. His father owned Bardon Hill Quarries, but on his mother's side he was related to the Fielding-Johnsons, the leading textile manufacturing family in Leicester. Everard was married to Mary Nutt from Newtown Unthank, one of four pretty sisters who all wed officers in the Leicestershire Regiment. He is remembered as being well educated, having studied at Cambridge, though he had left without taking his degree. He could be outspoken and somewhat eccentric, but to those who knew him well he was regarded as a loyal friend. A fellow officer, Peter Moore, wrote of Everard after his death in 1993:

> Richard was one of the bravest men I have ever met – anyone who saw him in action will tell you the same. He became a legendary figure in the battalion and his officers and men would have followed him anywhere. He was not reckless with the lives of his men, but he was totally unconcerned for his own life. He was decisive, unflappable and inspiring.[8]

Everard himself remembered:

> I left the Officer Cadet Training Unit (OCTU) in February 1940 and joined the battalion in March 1940 when they were stationed in Leicester

... After a short period in a recruit company I joined B Company commanded by Captain G.S. Gee ... The other officer in the company was Eric Capron, who joined the battalion the same day as myself.[9]

Capron was from Grimsby in Lincolnshire, and in peacetime a trawler owner. He soon became popular, with a dour sense of humour and a reputation for plain speaking. Captain Geoff Gee had been with the battalion considerably longer and assumed command of B Company in March 1940, when he relinquished the role of Adjutant. He lived near Uppingham, and in peacetime he worked for the family firm of Stead & Simpson, shoe manufacturers. He is remembered with affection by brother officers who knew him. One wrote:

He was a delightful man, well read and widely travelled ... Geoff seemed to be smiling broadly most of the time as if life in the army was almost farcical if it had not been so serious. He had a very dry sense of humour, but was extremely efficient in a rather laid back way ... Geoff was quite a lot older than the rest of us, perhaps in his mid thirties or almost forty, but he was very fit and could march for miles with his peculiar springy gait.[10]

Other new officers were Major L. Sawyer DSO and Lieutenant R.F.J. O'Reilly, both Regular officers who joined the battalion in March 1940 from the 1st battalion, now stationed at Agra in India. O'Reilly would subsequently become A Company commander. The Quartermaster, Lieutenant Tom Hall, was a veteran of the First World War. He had served as a corporal with the old D Company at Coalville in 1928, and was later commissioned. Lieutenant Cecil Botibol was from North London. Before the war he had served in the ranks of the Honourable Artillery Company, which had a long tradition of providing officers for other units, and before long Botibol, or 'Bot' as he was known, was commissioned into the Tigers. After attending a weapon training course he became the battalion Weapon Training Officer, and later became battalion Intelligence Officer. A Sephardi Jew, he was a member of the highly regarded Bevis Marks Synagogue congregation in London. His family was well known for importing cigars and other luxury goods. After his death, his obituary notice recorded that: 'Many of his brother officers will always hold the fondest memories of other off duty occasions spent in his delightful and ever generous company. He was generous to a degree, and many will long remember the super cigars that he invariably produced through the kindness of an uncle in the trade.'[11]

The winter of 1939–40 found the battalion occupying billets around Leicester. New recruits began to arrive and the battalion grew in strength. Former Private J.L. 'Moe' Harper of Leicester remembered:

I was a conscript, not a volunteer. There was approximately 100 of us, had to report to Gibraltar Barracks in Leeds, where we were given a medical, kitted out, given a hot meal and shipped straight back to Leicester, finishing up in an empty factory on the Eastern Boulevard alongside the river across the road. The first job I remember was digging slit trenches along the bank. We never used them. The cookhouse was in the factory garages at the back in Rydal Street.

We were divided up into four squads. There was already some personnel in the factory in uniform, as far as I can remember they were TA and Regular Army as quite a few were NCOs from Palestine & India as they were wearing the ribbons … Others were youngish lads … they were too young to go overseas and did not go to France with us.

We were called an 'intake', as were others who joined us later. The first time we heard the 2/5 Leicesters mentioned as our unit was sometime in January [1940] when we were up to battalion strength. It was pretty chaotic during this time, as we had hardly any military transport, using civvy trucks, just like 'Dad's Army' on TV.

Training in Leicester [included] plenty of toughening up Route Marches & PT. Route Marches (sometimes in snow) to Bradgate Park and its area. Sometimes wearing gas masks either going or coming back. Not very pleasant for 'new rookies'. We had marches to the Regimental Depot in Glen Parva for visits to the Gas Chamber. Before coming out, taking off our gasmasks to prove to us there was gas being used. One gas I remember was Phosgene, smelt like Pear Drops.

We were transported by any available transport to the firing ranges at Kibworth for Rifle and Machine Gun training and grenade throwing, bayonet practice etc. The Regular Army NCOs did not think much to us conscripts, they were always telling us they would make real soldiers of us!! No printable comments on that one.

Apart from being in Leicester and able to get home almost every evening, we had to be back in the factory by 2359 hours or we would be put on fatigues (jankers). As numbers increased we were split up and moved our billets to the City football ground, the Tigers rugby ground and the County Cricket ground. We still had to march back to the factory for meals, as the cookhouse stayed where it was. We did have a Salvation Army canteen in Jarrom Street quite close to our factory, and they did look after us very well.[12]

One of those who excelled on the range at Kibworth was Private Horace 'Jim' Greasley. He had grown up on a farm at Ibstock, and as a child had shot rabbits and other game for the pot using a small-bore rifle. He was a natural marksman and conversion to the .303 Short Magazine Lee-Enfield rifle was no great effort for him. In peacetime his shooting abilities might have taken him a long way within the regiment. In the forthcoming battles in France, however, he was to get precious few opportunities to put his skills into practice.

Don French of Kibworth was called up in December of 1939, and was instructed to report for duty on 10 January 1940 along with 'Moe' Harper. He remembered:

I went from Kibworth – it were a train that started at Northampton and picked up at every station to Loughborough. We went up to Leeds, had a plate of stew, and signed your name ... You got all your uniform and kit – it was here you are, here you are, they weren't worried about whether it fit you or not! ... They found a chap to call a sergeant, and another a corporal ... He [the sergeant] then had to bring a hundred of us back to Leicester. We were back in Leicester at ten past seven on this night, 10th of January. Me and the girlfriend – wife she is now – were going to the Opera House, you know to see the show they have on over Christmas. We had to give the tickets to her two sisters, they went, you know because I'd been called up, but I was back in Leicester in time to see them go![13]

At this time Don French's A Company were still in the shoe factory on Eastern Boulevard, where he joined them, but not long afterwards they moved for more intensive training to the Filbert Street ground of Leicester City Football Club. He recalled:

It was alright on there, we had hot water to wash with. We were in the dressing rooms. [The rest of the battalion] were in billets up the road, where you go into the city. B Company came back there then, and where we slept they had to have that for the canteen then, for getting the meals ready, because they'd got double the amount of people.[14]

Training at the City football ground was still rudimentary in many respects:

> We used to march from one goal post to another ... we'd got a rifle, but
> it was from 1917 ... 3704 was the number on it – it was worn out years
> ago! We never had any ammunition to practise with; we never had any
> ammunition to put in it. Marching, that was all, we used to go on route
> marches, they used to reckon you wanted to go about twenty-five miles
> before you knew you'd been on one! They were round and about
> Leicester, sometimes to Wigston or other places. They knew where they
> were going because the NCOs were only ordinary soldiers, reservists,
> called up, given a couple of stripes and put in charge of us. [They were] all
> chaps that had been out to India, done their time and been on the reserve.
> They called them up and gave them two stripes.[15]

Joe Kynoch was soon to leave the 2nd/5th to join its sister 1st/5th battalion,
but before he did so he spent a few months in the company of Harper, French
and Greasley. He remembered:

> [My] billets were in Havelock Street in Leicester and we were paid the
> nominal sum of ten shillings a week, or fifty pence in today's money,
> whilst we were there and with cigarettes at twenty for five new pence and
> beer at two-and-a-half pence a pint, we didn't have much by the way of
> change in our pockets by the next day, especially if we had been home on a
> weekend pass or even to the 'flicks'.
>
> Most of us smoked in those days and because we didn't have a lot to do
> we soon got through twenty cigarettes in a day, also, we discovered pretty
> quickly that if we couldn't afford to drink beer then we had to drink cider
> at just about half the price and it was really potent.
>
> It was because of drinking this brew with my mates in the local that I
> became ill in the billet one night and was put on a charge by the Orderly
> Corporal and had to do my first spell of jankers the following day peeling
> potatoes in the cookhouse.
>
> During those early days of mobilisation we always seemed to be on
> parade for some reason or another and if it wasn't for drawing kit it would
> almost certainly be for an update of injections or perhaps a dental
> parade.[16]

The battalion was fortunate in having two senior NCOs with an enormous
amount of military experience between them. Indeed, both of these men had
been decorated with the Distinguished Conduct Medal in the First World

War. They were Regimental Sergeant Major Edwin Ross and Regimental Quartermaster Sergeant Joe French. Ross was a Londoner who had joined the Leicestershire Regiment under age at the beginning of the First World War. He had seen action in France with the 2nd battalion at the battles of Neuve Chapelle and Loos before moving with his battalion to Mesopotamia. Here he had been awarded the DCM for carrying messages under fire. Working his way through the ranks, in 1936 he was posted as senior Permanent Staff Instructor to the 4th Leicesters. When that unit was converted to an Anti-Aircraft battalion he stayed with them as Company Sergeant Major and Instructor. He retired from the Army in August 1939 and became the caretaker of Ulverscroft Road TA drill hall, the headquarters of the 44th Anti Aircraft battalion. However, within a short period of time he returned to the Colours, answering an appeal for ex-Warrant Officers to rejoin. He was then posted to the fledgling 2nd/5th battalion. Joe French, meanwhile, had served with the 1st battalion in the First World War and had been in France from 1914 to 1918. He was awarded the DCM for bravery during the final Allied offensive in 1918.

Late in 1939 a detachment from the 2nd/5th was sent to Derby to guard the Rolls Royce aircraft factory, which was felt to be vulnerable not just to attack by the enemy, but also to possible sabotage by the IRA. Among the members of this detachment was Leonard Bingley, a hosiery warehouseman from Leicester, and now a lance corporal in B Company. One of his letters, dated 26 November 1939, survives and captures a sense of the monotony of this kind of duty, not to mention the bitter cold in winter. He writes to his wife:

Thank you very much for the [balaclava] helmet which I received Sat. It will be very nice and warm. I was surprised that you got it finished so quickly it was a very pleasant surprise ... I don't know if you have got very far with my gloves, but I am pleased to say I have found the others again in a very peculiar way. It was like this: one Friday night I was on guard and one of the fellows asked me if I had any mittens (the army supply these for us) and I said that I had not, and he said that I could borrow his gloves, and he would send me some mittens out. Well he pulled his gloves out his pocket, and lo and behold – they were mine so I promptly told him that they belonged to me and that I had lost them some time ago. He never said anything, so I just took them, and that was that! I am very pleased that I found them again, for I valued them very much. So if you have not got very far with another pair, perhaps you could leave them and knit me a pullover ... it is wet and cold here, not very pleasant at all, but it might be worse. I am glad you have got the tree out again for the children, when I come home I will bring something for them, because they say we are having our bounty on Monday, its about time we had it, we have been kept waiting long enough for it ain't we … I am on guard at the moment, and it is about 11.15 and I have got to go for my dinner at 12.30 … I am on guard at 1 o'clock and come off at 3.00, so I can write some more after and catch the 6.30 post. The last time I was on guard the lady of the billet put me a flask of hot tea on the front doorstep, and I had it at 1 o'clock at night, and you can imagine how it went down at that time in the night … Have you heard any more from Klynton yet, I hope they don't intend to stop your allowance. By the way did you copy out the letter that I wrote [to them]? … Just at the moment someone is playing the piano, and the tune is one that suits my mood – it goes like this – 'If I could but hold your charms again in my arms, then life would be complete.' I am thinking just the same thing all the time but everything will come out right in the end for us both you see … I went to the pictures last night, Saturday, and got a good seat for 6*d*, but I did not care for the pictures much …[17]

Bingley's letter seems to imply that his wife was claiming some sort of separation allowance from her husband's pre-war employer, the hosiery firm Klynton-Davies in Leicester, while the bounty to which he refers was payable to Territorial troops by the government upon mobilisation. It seems that nearly three months after the start of the war, the 2nd/5th Leicesters had yet to receive theirs. In March 1940 this detachment was relieved and returned to Leicester. A further detachment was found to guard Cottesmore aerodrome, whilst on 11 March 1940 the battalion provided a firing party, buglers and pall bearers for the funeral of Lieutenant Colonel T.P. Fielding-Johnson, late of the Leicestershire Regiment.

Despite the fact that the battalion was still little more than a holding formation for new recruits, and that although it existed at battalion strength really only on paper (being deficient in heavy weapons and transport) political events were about to intervene to throw the 2nd/5th Leicesters directly into the path of Hitler's blitzkrieg. On Friday, 26 April 1940 at 0120 hours the battalion left Leicester LMS railway station in two parties. By 0300 hours they were in Southampton and embarked upon the requisitioned Isle of Man Steam Packet passenger vessel *Viking*, bound for Brittany. Britain was committed under the terms of her alliance with the French to send twelve divisions to

France should war with Germany break out. In spite of the parlous state of the British Army (the best formations of which were still in garrisons around the world such as India and the Middle East) this commitment was fulfilled, by agreeing to send a number of untrained Territorial divisions on the tacit understanding that they would only be used for the construction of defensive works until such time as they were fully trained. For the troops that made up these so-called 'digging divisions',[18] most of whom came from the Midlands and Yorkshire, this was seen as nothing more than an addition to the annual Territorial summer camps – an extended summer holiday in the French sunshine with a little work thrown in. This dodge allowed the Secretary of State for War, the Right Honourable Leslie Hore-Belisha MP, to tell the House of Commons that Britain had fulfilled her military commitment to France. In total warfare, however, there can be no sitting on the sidelines and watching as spectators. The boiling cauldron of war was about to overflow, and draw the 2nd/5th Leicesters into its fulminating heart.

Chapter 2

To Join the Fray

The men of the new British Expeditionary Force (BEF) began to arrive in France in October 1939, and it was not just their title that was an eerie reminder of their forebears in the First World War. The troops immediately began digging in and preparing strong defensive positions. For those who could remember it, the whole affair was more than a little reminiscent of 1918. This was the period of the so-called 'Phoney War', a phrase coined by an American journalist. Nazi dictator Adolf Hitler still harboured hopes of reaching a political accord with Britain. This would leave him a free hand to deal with matters in the east, and he was not in quite as strong a position as he would have liked others to believe, in spite of his aggressive rhetoric. His navy was dwarfed by that of Britain, and even if their tanks and planes were easily outclassed by those of the Germans, the French still possessed more of both. If the French had decided to attack whilst the bulk of Hitler's forces were still occupied in Poland in 1939, the course of the Second World War might have been very different. Yet the French Army as a whole was riven by poor morale and defeatism, and their generals were elderly men fixated upon defence above all other doctrines. The French military elite was so utterly traumatised by the losses of the First World War that any offensive action on its part was out of the question. Politically also, France had been deeply divided in the 1930s. Communists and socialists had battled with each other to lead the opposition to a powerful right wing which threatened to become a dangerous Fifth Column should France ever find herself at war with the fascist powers of Europe. The British people were undoubtedly reluctant to go to war in 1939, remembering only too well the horrors of 1914–18, but the French public had even less stomach for the fight, and many Frenchmen openly welcomed the prospect of German domination as the answer to France's problems.

For the moment at least then, there was no movement in the west. Britain and France, meanwhile, made for uneasy allies. As far as the British Army was concerned, if the trenches were a reminder of 1918, that was as far as the parallel went. In 1918 the British Expeditionary Force had reigned supreme on the Western Front. In terms of equipment, tactics and training, by the end of the First World War the British Army was the most efficient it had ever been. The Army of 1939 by contrast was a mere shadow of that which had swept the Germans before it twenty years previously. The limitations in defence spending in the 1920s, and more particularly the 1930s as the Great Depression bit into the nation's finances, had left the Army woefully unprepared for any future conflict. Furthermore, Britain's re-armament when finally faced with the new German threat in the late 1930s had been hampered by the official policy of appeasement toward Hitler. What resources were available had largely gone to re-equip the RAF and in 1939 Major General (later Field Marshal) Bernard Montgomery had stated bluntly that the British Regular Army was unfit to take part in any sort of realistic exercise, let alone take on a first-class European enemy.

In the field, the British in 1940 were led by Field Marshal Lord Gort VC. Unquestionably a fearless junior commander, Gort had won the supreme award for bravery in command of an infantry battalion in 1918. It was doubtful, however, if he really had the strategic overview necessary to make the transition to effective senior commander, and certainly when the German attack on France did come, he appeared as though a rabbit caught in the headlights of an oncoming car. The press dubbed him 'Tiger' Gort in an effort to bolster his public persona, but it fooled few and Gort never held senior command again after the debacle in France. Only the Germans (notably their commanders Heinz Guderian and Erwin Rommel) had in the 1930s fully absorbed the potential of the tank to transform the battlefield; the British and French still had little clear idea of the best way to deploy infantry and armour together. Yet the BEF, woefully short of guns, effective tanks and trained men, had one advantage over the Germans that might just prove to be crucial in the coming fight: in the 1930s they had done away with horses, becoming an entirely mechanised army, even if this meant that the actual motorised transport sometimes took the form of requisitioned laundry vans. Leaving aside the lightning punch of the blitzkrieg, Hitler's army still moved at the speed of the draught horse, meaning his panzer armies could easily outrun their supply lines and were often forced to halt.

Regardless of Britain's weakness, in 1939 Leslie Hore-Belisha, Secretary of State for War, had publicly committed Britain to send nineteen divisions to France should war break out. In spite of Hore-Belisha's ambitious claims, once war was declared it became apparent that the Army was simply not in a position to fulfil this obligation. However, mounting pressure from the French, coupled with an urgent need to construct field fortifications, led to a compromise decision to send three untrained and effectively unarmed Territorial Army divisions to France – the 12th, 23rd and 46th. To the British they were known as the 'digging divisions'. The Germans, when they eventually came up against them, nicknamed them 'Kinderdivizionen', or children's divisions, because of the high number of 19-year-old conscripts in their ranks. There was at the beginning, however, no expectation whatsoever that these formations were to do anything other than 'coolie work' in France, and thus they left behind in England any divisional artillery or signals formations that they might have had.

Thus it was that in April 1940, the 2nd/5th battalion of the Leicestershire Regiment stepped on to the stage in France, the battalion being sent there purportedly for training as well as labouring duties. The 2nd/5th Leicesters, 2nd/5th Sherwood Foresters and 9th Sherwood Foresters together comprised the 139th Brigade, itself part of the 46th Division. It was envisaged by the high command that the brigade would be engaged in building a railway siding, with two battalions training and a third working at any one time. The Leicesters began the work, but were never to receive their training.

The advance party had left England on 14 April under the command of Captain Sidney Brown and reached Cherbourg early the following day. After drawing stores at Renaix on 17 April, they proceeded to the Breton village of L'Hermitage, where they began construction work to bring the site up to the required standard for a battalion. Nissen huts were assembled in a pleasant orchard and supplies were stockpiled for the battalion. On 22 April a further advance party of ten men under Lieutenant David North arrived to assist, fortuitously as it turned out, as Brown was given compassionate leave to visit his father in Leicester who was reported to be seriously ill. The full battalion finally left Leicester in the early hours of 26 April.

Richard Everard remembered:

We made a rather furtive exit from Leicester, leaving in the very early hours of one April morning, and went by train down to Southampton. Our advance party had already gone ahead, but we did not know exactly where, at least I did not. We embarked early in the morning and spent a day and night waiting in Southampton Water and eventually sailed at night. We awoke next morning to find a French plane escorting us and our ship steaming into Cherbourg harbour. After the usual delays attendant on the disembarking of a large number of men and stores we boarded a train which took us near to Rennes in the centre of Brittany. We detrained and after a short march we arrived at a camp which was already prepared for us.[1]

After a long winter of training in the somewhat dreary surroundings of industrial Leicester, it was with some optimism that the battalion approached this new phase. Shortly before leaving England it had been announced that Colonel E.C. Atkins DL had been pleased to accept the position of Honorary Colonel of the battalion – a sure sign that it was approaching a certain standard of readiness, though there was still a great deal to be done. The weather had also turned now and the balmy conditions in this picturesque part of France contributed to the general ambiance. Soon most of the men were tanned and fit, which was just as well given the ordeal that they were soon to endure. The countryside was flat and wooded, dotted with orchards that produced good local Breton cider. This and the red wine available in the estaminets were greatly enjoyed by officers and men alike, and after the daily toil was completed there were other amusements in the form of concerts or football.

The battalion's main task was the construction of a railway siding, which would facilitate the moving of artillery ammunition from a nearby munitions dump. Many of the men remembered the sheer physical effort of securing hooks around sections of steel railway track, hoisting them up on chains, fitting them on to sleepers by hammering in iron spikes and then building up the ballast around them by shovelling in tons of gravel. Everard continues:

It was obvious to all of us that the higher command did not intend to use our division for fighting. We had come to France to do Pioneer work and to do what training we could. None of the divisional artillery had come over with us. We had no carriers or 3″ mortars in the battalion, no signal equipment, wireless or telephones. Our sole signal resources were two Despatch Riders (Don Rs) Private Hatts and Private Wilson . . . In each Company we had three Bren guns and one Anti-tank (A/T) rifle and no 2″ Mortars. The official establishment for these weapons being respectively nine, three and three. We also had very little transport. We did not think there was anything very wrong in this but it did have a bearing on future events.[2]

Whilst the battalion was at L'Hermitage the *Green Tiger* recorded the arrival of a new officer: 'One night, at about midnight, the peaceful slumbers of the commanding officer and Second-in-Command were rudely disturbed by the clattering footsteps of an intruder. After their volley of expletives had died down, he announced himself; and thus it was quite unexpectedly that we acquired as our Adjutant Lieutenant J.W.B. Marshall.[3]

John Marshall was a Regular officer, educated at Uppingham School and Sandhurst. Commissioned in 1936, he had previously served with the 2nd battalion of the Leicestershire Regiment in Londonderry and Palestine. He was remembered by those who knew him as a highly efficient officer with a pleasant manner. It was said he often liked to conceal his capacity for hard work and clear thinking behind an assumed casual 'haven't a clue' demeanour. He quickly took on the role of company commander as well as adjutant, and would be a great asset to the battalion in the trying time that lay ahead.

For Gordon Spring, meanwhile, life in France was grand. He remembered one incident with particular amusement:

Our cook was a First World War veteran and we had old coppers [to cook in] . . . it was my job to keep the hot water topped up. By mistake I put cold water in and the pudding sank to the bottom. This cook ran after me with a cleaver: 'I'm gunna chop your f*****g head off', he shouted at me . . . [I had] bought this lovely plate with the intentions of eating my supper off it. [Later] Cook said: 'How many spuds tonight, Spring?' I answered: 'Two'. He then banged them on my plate and broke it. 'Got yer, yer little bastard', he said.[4]

For the Leicesters the first inkling that all was not well in France came when Lieutenant Marshall was awoken at 0200 hours one morning to attend a brigade conference. At this he was informed that the German attack on France and the Low Countries had erupted with frightening speed. The Germans were now moving faster than anyone had dared imagine and were sweeping all before them.

The fateful initiative that turned the 46th Division from a labour force into a fighting force came from its commanding officer, Major General Harry Curtis. When the overly optimistic Curtis blithely announced that his men were fit and ready to take their place in the line as fighting troops, British General Headquarters, hitherto gripped by paralysis, seized at his offer and the 46th were propelled headlong into the melee. Young, inexperienced and poorly equipped, the men of the division were to be expended in order to buy time to allow better equipped formations to escape.

The 2nd/5th battalion was now placed at twelve hours' notice to move. The seriousness of the situation had not, however, become apparent to the officers

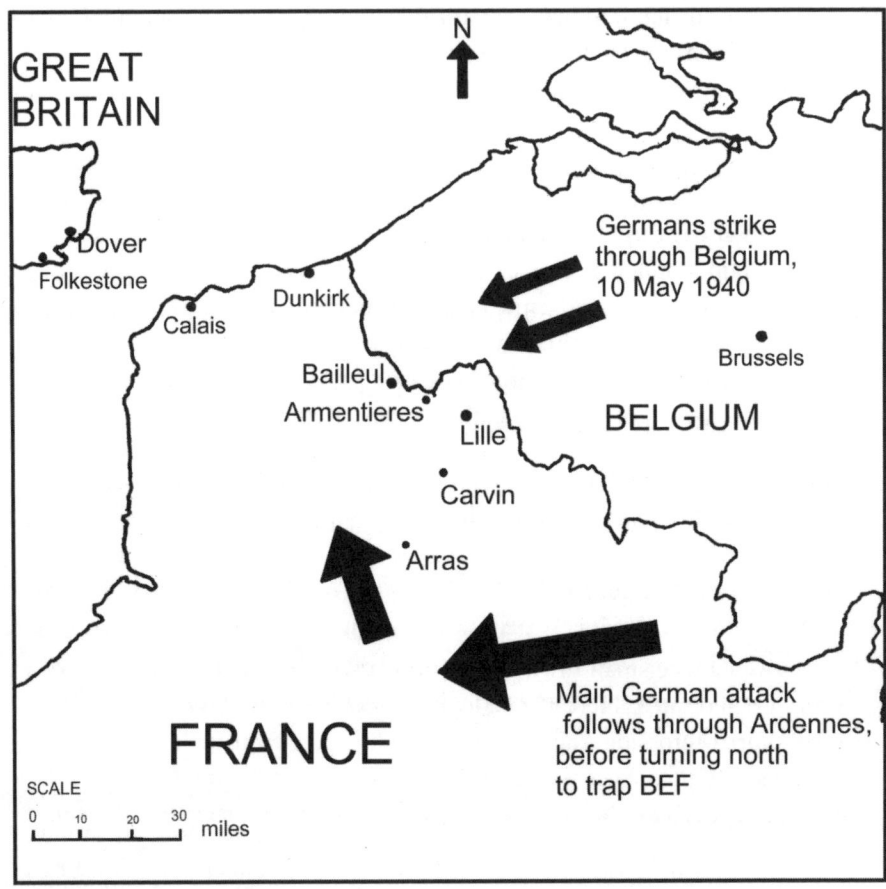

France and Belgium, May 1940.

and men themselves, as evidenced by the fact that among the mass of equipment and stores loaded on to lorries space was found for officers' deck-chairs and the battalion band instruments! By 1400 hours on 15 May the men of the battalion were aboard trucks to take them into Rennes, where, with the 2nd/5th Foresters, they boarded trains bound for the front.

The journey on the train was crowded and unpleasant – little had changed on the French *Chemin de Fer* since the days of the First World War when the fathers of these men had travelled in carriages similarly marked '8 cheval 40 hommes'. Gordon Spring remembered:

> Lying on straw, [crammed in] a wagon, bully beef and biscuits all day long was how I would describe that journey. Little did I know that we would be

on the train for days. When we passed stations I got off for a crap, had a wash and then got back on. The big carriage doors were rolled back at mealtimes.[5]

Private Victor Clough remembered the battalion's introduction to war as they moved up through Belgium to the Albert Canal:

The balloon went up, the breakthrough, and they shoved us all on a train, and the train stopped at a place called Nederbrakel. We got off the train, and we turned around and came back and suddenly there was some Stukas came over and the next thing we seen was a platform flying up in the air that was bombed. Then we came back we sort of formed up and there was one farm – we'd got rather a military type Regimental Sergeant Major named Ross – we were at this farm, a headquarters, and he made everyone take their cap badges off, and throw them in a well, and all the [personal] papers that they had got on them were destroyed ...[6]

Richard Everard remembered his first and probably only meeting with the genial General Curtis:

We arrived at the small town of Seclin just short of the Belgium frontier, where we detrained. Here after a longish wait we transferred to trucks and were shortly crossing the Belgium border, past anti-tank ditches and defences that had been laboriously dug during the winter, and whose protection the army left by sallying into Belgium to meet the advancing Germans. We passed through Tournai which had already been damaged by bombing. Just short of Renaix, 'B' Company was de-bussed and whilst Geoff [Gee] went into the town with the CO to do a 'recce', I got our cooks busy on preparing breakfast. While we were there the Divisional General and his G1 Lt Col Chichester-Constable DSO (soon to become our Brigadier) came by on foot and stopped to ask how we were. This may seem a commonplace but it is the small things like that which make a General liked by his troops. He becomes to them not a vague figurehead but a human being.[7]

At Seclin the firepower of the battalion was boosted – on paper at least – by the issue of a further fourteen Boys Anti-tank rifles. A bolt-action rifle fed from a five-shot magazine, the weapon was large and heavy, with a bipod at the front and a separate grip below the padded butt. In order to combat the recoil caused by the large 0.55 inch (13.9mm) round, the barrel was mounted on a slide, and a shock absorber was fitted to the bipod along with a muzzle brake on the barrel. The Boys had been designed with numerous small narrow-slotted screws of soft steel set very tight into the body of the weapon, and its repair and maintenance proved a nightmare for British ordnance-repair crews. Despite its recoil slide and cushioned buttpad, the felt recoil of the weapon (along with noise and muzzle blast) when fired was terrific, frequently causing neck strains and bruised shoulders. This made it a deeply unpopular rifle and in consequence the Boys was almost never fired as a free weapon (i.e. not affixed to a support) except in emergencies. A bigger problem for the men of the 2nd/5th Leicesters, however, was the shortage of ammunition to use with it, and it was this rather than concerns about the recoil that really limited its effectiveness.

The task of the battalion was now to keep the roads clear of refugees and to act as lines of communication troops, guarding the roads and directing military traffic. On 18 May, their first day on this duty, they encountered the British 1st Division returning in trucks from four days of heavy fighting in the Brussels area. Both the drivers and the occupants of the trucks had the look of men who have been in combat and without sleep for several days. The drivers had no clear idea of where they were going and different units were intermixed but troops under Company Quartermaster Sergeant Higgs did sterling work as traffic policemen, trying to sort them out.

An additional problem was posed by the hoards of refugees who were also now pouring out of Belgium, trying to escape the bombing around Brussels. The refugees made for a pitiable sight, carrying all their worldly possessions with them. It was said that turning the refugees out on to the roads was part of the German plan in order to obstruct the movement of military traffic – if so, it was certainly working as the Leicesters spent much of their time ushering these people to the sides of the congested roads in order to let military traffic through. However, stories of Fifth Columnists stirring up panic and deliberately encouraging these people to take to the roads probably had as much validity as the spy scares of 1914.

In common with the rest of the BEF, orders were soon received to fall back and the men of the Leicesters began their own long and weary march along the pavé of the French roads, stopping along the way to cook breakfast. Both officers and men were still very naïve about the reality of war, in spite of what they had seen so far. Richard Everard remembered:

We soon found a cottage where the people were very kind and insisted on us coming in and drinking coffee with them. I remember the old grandmother saying 'pauvre soldat', and I wondered why. I was really rather enjoying myself; but I have no doubts now that the good lady had been through 1914–18 and knew a good deal more about war than I did.[8]

Furthermore, to men in the ranks such as Don French over the days that followed it began to appear as if the officers knew little more than their men about what the role of the battalion was to be, or indeed where they would be moving to next, or why. Very often the movements of the battalion followed no logical pattern and after completing a move, often the first orders received would be to move again.

On 19 May B Company was found on the line of march, in single file by the side of the road so as to present as small a target as possible to enemy aircraft, which marauded across the skies unmolested – or so it seemed to the ordinary British Tommy at any rate. The weather was getting hotter now, and made life uncomfortable for the men marching in thick khaki serge battledress. Sweat formed under the rubber liners of their tin hats and trickled down their faces as they slogged along, but often moving by truck was simply too difficult with the roads crowded with refugees – and also too dangerous with the constant threat of air attack.

As the men approached a village in the distance, the now familiar throb-throb of aeroplane engines could be heard overhead. As they drew nearer the source of the noise became apparent. Some thirty German bombers were circling and preparing to attack the village, which must have contained a brigade headquarters or similar. The company dispersed into the long grass by the sides of the road until the enemy bombers had done their work and disappeared. Resuming their march the men were given a grim introduction to the reality of modern warfare as they passed the shattered village, with stretcher bearers attending to the wounded. The march took them on to Toufflers where they rendezvoused with the rest of the battalion. Richard Everard takes up the story:

We got the men off the road under cover and very soon there was a good meal ready for everybody ... I remember seeing [Lieutenant] David White gazing ruefully at his feet. For some reason best known to himself, he had been marching in gum boots. Anyone who has marched for over ten miles on a hot day in rubber boots will know the reason for his anguish. About 5.00pm the whole battalion moved on again for another two hours until we reached a crossroads where we met the Foresters. We dispersed and rested.[9]

Whilst the battalion was resting, motor transport was due to arrive to pick them up and take them on to Ancoisne. Typically in the chaos of those days nothing arrived, so eventually as it was just getting dark, it was decided to continue the march until at 2200 hours the battalion reached the deserted town of Lesquin. Here, billets were found in an abandoned factory and a school. Everard was one of those in the school and remembered:

> Everyone was very tired, and after sentries had been posted, we tried to sleep. It was very cold on the stone schoolroom floors. Eric [Capron] and I tried to make ourselves comfortable with two gas capes; it was not a great success and I was glad when morning came. I went outside as soon as it was light and found the inevitable tea being brewed by the RSM [Ross]. I sometimes think that if it had not been for tea we should never have won the war.[10]

On 20 May the battalion was on the move again. Their destination this time was Emmerin, near Lille, which was easily within marching distance. However, they were ordered to wait for motor transport, which was late in arriving. When it did eventually turn up, the officer in charge misread his maps and the column got lost. Another aspect of the battalion's ill-preparedness was its paucity of good reliable maps. Captain Brown records in his notes the fact that he had no compass and the map that he was issued with was very small scale, with half the roads not shown. On 20 May he was forced to confer with an Anti Aircraft battery and asked to see their map, whilst two days previously there had been a similar occurrence when he had approached a Royal Army Service Corps column in order to consult their large-scale map. This, however, was a problem not confined simply to the 2nd/5th Leicesters. Maps were in short supply across the BEF as a whole and those that were available were often out of date. France had not been surveyed properly since the middle of the nineteenth century, and often the most up-to-date maps available were those produced by the British Army in the First World War.

Having finally got the men on the move in the right direction, Brown and his troops were machine-gunned and forced to scatter by a German bomber in the village of Valenciennes. They were cheered, however, by the sight of the enemy machine brought down by a posse of Spitfires. Later, the battalion was again attacked by German aircraft, this time three Messerschmidts, which fired their machine guns at them but did not cause any casualties. It was late in the afternoon before the battalion reached its destination, the town of Emmerin, but billets were soon found for the men and cooks got to work on an evening meal.

The following day, 21 May, the men were roused early for their breakfasts. All non-essential kit was to be left there – a clear sign that action was imminent – and a party was told off to look after it, comprising Lieutenant Cliff Marriott, Sergeant Terry (a former employee of the Grand Hotel in Leicester) and a few other men. At about 9.00am the men trudged off through the battle-damaged streets, once again in single file in order to minimise casualties should they come under air attack. Everard takes up the story once more:

> About midday we passed through Seclin, and had a short halt on the out-skirts of the town. We found a largish house nearby which had a superbly stocked cellar. I had never seen anything like it before. Tier upon tier of champagne, burgundy and other wines whose names I cannot remember. It seemed foolish to leave it all to be drunk by the Germans, so we decided to help ourselves. We gave everybody in 'B' Company a good drink of red wine and piled enough champagne on the Company truck to give everyone a pint each with the evening meal.[11]

In fact that night's meal was prepared in the surroundings of the Bois des Flines, a large wood close to the village of Le Boujie. HQ Company had the worst bivouac site, close to a stagnant pool of water and as a consequence that company suffered very badly from mosquito bites. Here, after a meal of local poultry cooked in an abandoned cottage and washed down with finest quality champagne, B Company settled down contentedly to rest for the night. How-ever, this was not to be, as at midnight B Company men were roused from their slumbers and were on the move again – a short march to rendezvous with their Royal Army Service Corps motor transport and they were on the road once more – to take over defensive positions from another battalion. At about 0400 hours on 22 May they arrived at Marchiennes, which had been very badly damaged by bombing, and then took up positions in the south of the town along the banks of the River Scharpe.

Everard continues his narrative:

> I put my platoon in position along the canal bank and fixed my HQ in a house slightly back from the canal but in the middle of the position we were to hold. It was by now almost light and I went to contact a gunner officer who had an observation point in the church tower. He told me what he knew about the locality which was not very much. The Germans

were somewhere over the canal but where and in what numbers he did not know. He advised me to keep a good air look-out as the town was usually strafed pretty frequently during the day. When I got back to my platoon it was quite light and I could see the whole position clearly. The town was very badly damaged. My house was on the right hand side of a road leading to a bridge over the canal. The bridge had been partially blown and was impassable for vehicles but it would have been an easy matter to cross it on foot. So I assumed my task was to guard that bridge and I left my platoon as I had originally placed them on the canal bank on both sides of the bridge. I was expecting a company of our battalion to come and take over during the morning but nobody came and I had no idea who was meant to be on my left and right. We had a visit from German bombers and got our Bren gun in action but with no result.[12]

In fact, the Bren was probably the most effective weapon the Tommies of the 2nd/5th battalion possessed. Lighter and less clumsy than the Boys Anti-tank rifle and more modern than the bolt-action Lee-Enfields, in trained hands it was a fearsome weapon. Capable of both single-shot action and also fully automatic fire, it was to become a mainstay of the British Army in Europe, the Mediterranean and the Far East. When it was first introduced to the British Army just before the war, soldiers complained that it was too accurate – the 'cone' of fire that it produced was too tight to knock down a line of enemy soldiers, and so it had to be adapted to produce a wider spread of fire. In trained hands it was very effective. The few that the battalion possessed were allocated to the best shots and the most experienced soldiers.

On 22 May the commanding officer Lieutenant Colonel Ruddle and the commanders of the rifle companies departed for a conference, leaving the battalion under the temporary command of Captain Sidney Brown. He recorded in his notebook that HQ Company:

Marched through Flines-les-Raches & shortly after leaving had to take cover when enemy aircraft arrived. About 1300 hours we arrived at our destination. On the road outside was a convoy of old French buses. Very soon these were bombed, most of the bombs falling near us, but 3 vehicles were fired & there were a few casualties among the French. Our Brens fired but met with no success. About 1400 hrs the CO returned & shortly after we moved to take up positions. My coy was in reserve & we marched through Marchiennes to Elpret. Found village full of French veterinary corps but finally got billets. Coy HQ in quite decent house. 2 roast chickens for supper & slept on a bed for a change. Quiet night.[13]

Everard, meanwhile, ordered his men to get down to similar matters during the lull:

There were a few hungry looking dogs prowling about in the ruins [of Marchiennes]. The day wore on. Still no news from the battalion. We were lucky in finding a good store of food left in the house by the previous company and we had stew and char for the midday meal. Shortly after this a very smartly dressed French officer came up to me and started to ask all sorts of questions about our positions and what troops there were in our area. He said he was co-ordinating artillery support and had to know where everybody was. I was very guileless and told him all I knew; but looking back on those days I would not be surprised if he was a German in captured French uniform. I did not give him much information because I had not much to give. The afternoon wore on and still no news from the battalion.[14]

Confusion and lack of information from High Command were rapidly becoming the order of the day now. The men in the ranks were used to the fact that they knew very little about what was going on most of the time, and were told even less, but it was becoming apparent even to them that their junior officers were as ignorant as they were. Added to this was the mutual mistrust and misunderstanding between the British and French troops on the ground. Everard and his men were to exchange positions once again later that day:

In the late afternoon, Lieutenant O'Reilly arrived with 'C' Company and said he had come to take over the position and also told me where the rest of 'B' Company were. So I marched my platoon out and after an hour-and-a-half I found Geoff [Gee] and the rest of the company. We had a position in open country behind the same canal that ran through La Bassée. There was a farm house in an orchard about 200 yards back from the canal which . . . company HQ shared with a gunner observation officer. There was also one 2-pounder anti-tank gun in the orchard between the house and the canal. On our right was 'D' Company and on our left were some coloured troops, Moroccans . . . Although the battalion was very thinly spread out over five miles of the canal it did seem that we were going to have some chance of stabilising our line. So far all the moves had been very incomprehensible to us as we had not contacted the Germans at all and we had no news of how the rest of the fighting was going.

However we settled in on the assumption we were going to stay put. We had some of the Champagne left over from the previous night and a sheep and some chickens were killed for the pot and everybody had a good meal. Next morning, Geoff and I went out early in front of our positions to do a 'recce'. It was always best to do it this way if possible as you get a good idea of how the enemy would see things. On our way back we were shot at by a French soldier. Luckily his aim was bad. We felt confident we could hold our own here as the country was very flat and we had a fine field of fire and the Royal Artillery officer in his Observation Post in the farm could see for miles. But when we returned to Company HQ, we found the inevitable order to move. It was always the same. We were never in one place for more than a day. We all felt that if given a chance to stand and hold a position we could. I wonder?[15]

The following day, 23 May, dawned with unexpected drama when Captain Brown stood HQ Company to at first light. His first action of the day was to send Private H.J. Collins (a soldier from Fairfield Road, Market Harborough) and one of his comrades off on a foraging mission to try to find some milk on a nearby farm. The men returned empty-handed and lucky to be in one piece, having been fired upon by jumpy French troops in the vicinity of the farm.

At about 1000 hours the 2nd/5th battalion set off for that day's destination, the Fôret de Marchiennes, which they reached at about lunchtime. The wood, however, was found to contain a number of French troops and, more worryingly, a French ammunition dump. It was thus not the healthiest of places to bivouac when under imminent threat of air attack, and so was abandoned in favour of Bouvignies, to the west of the forest. At midnight, footsore and tired, the battalion was on the move again. This time it was heading to its final position as an organised battalion in the 1940 campaign – the defences of the La Bassée canal in the Carvin area – where many of its members were to meet their destiny in the days that lay ahead.

By 24 May, Field Marshal Gort was faced with the worsening military situation in France after the failure of his counterattack at Arras, which had momentarily shaken the Germans. Gort and his generals ordered the 139th Brigade and other mainly Territorial formations to take up position on what was known as the Canal Line. Put simply, after the initial German offensive in Belgium had drawn the British and French forward, the main German thrust by her panzer armies had punched a massive hole through the French Army in the weakly defended Ardennes sector further south. The Germans had then swung north in a sickle-shaped movement. This forced the Allies on to the defensive on two fronts. The British and French-held territory now resembled a corridor 70 miles long by 25 miles wide, with the open end at the top being the Channel coast around Dunkirk. The Canal Line thus formed the western edge of the corridor. This defensive line, which was intended to keep the corridor open as long as possible, made use of the series of canals that cut through the French coal-mining areas north of Arras. The canals had originally been built to serve the many pit heads that dotted this industrialised landscape, and they ran roughly north-west to south-east. Whilst the terrain north and east of the canals was predominantly urban, to the south and west were open fields interspersed by woodlands which would provide good cover for an attacking formation.

The Leicesters were now part of 'Mac Force' (a hastily put together composite formation). Their task was simply to hold their portion of line for as long as possible. In the space of a fortnight the role of the 46th Division had changed from that of a labour force, to lines of communication troops and now finally, in an act of desperation, they were to be thrown into the fray as a fighting formation. There was tacit acknowledgement from above that the Territorial divisions holding this line were to be sacrificed if necessary, in order to allow other units to escape.

On 24 May the 2nd/5th battalion de-bussed at the Bois d'Epinoy, not far from Carvin, from where the men marched into their allotted position along the Canal de la Haute Deule. The bridges across the canal had in most cases already been demolished by the Royal Engineers and French Army engineers, in an effort to impede the approaching Germans. The sector initially allotted to the battalion was some 7,000yd long, from Pont a Venin southwards almost to Oignies. These positions were held with A company at Pont a Vendin, B Company to the south-east, holding the footings of the destroyed bridge at Maudit, followed by HQ company facing Courrières, and finally D Company west of Oignies. C Company was in reserve. In the early hours of 24 May, Captain Brown and his subaltern Lieutenant Sharp set off to reconnoitre positions along the canal. Brown wrote later:

> Coy sector, East to West, Road bridge Oignies–Lens road exclusive to road & railway bridge Pont de Courriers inclusive … Position to be

occupied with French & bridges to be blown when required. Ground sloped up a little from the canal and then dead flat for over ¼ mile to Libercourt–Carvin road. No cover of any kind. Bridges blown 1100–1200 hours by order of French. Coy arrived & started taking up positions about 1400 hrs. No tools for digging to begin with. Later some arrived about 1730 and digging began in earnest. Equipment was four Brens & 5 anti-tank rifles so decided on four weapon pits & was able to give each a good field of fire. Coy HQ was situated around three haystacks about 200 yards back from the canal. During the afternoon a German bomber came over Coy HQ low down & we used our only weapon, rifle fire. It passed over the canal where it was met by a little more fire from the French & then came down with plenty of smoke in a field behind some houses. Were we successful or the French?[16]

Such a long front would have been difficult to hold anyway, but at about 1700 hours on 24 May, fresh orders were received for the battalion to take over more of the canal, this time running north from Pont a Vendin towards Salome. In order to effect this manouevre as quickly as possible, C Company were dispatched directly to the northern end of the battalion line in the Salome area. B Company was withdrawn to Carvin to become the reserve. B Company's position at Pont Maudit was taken over by HQ Company, which sent Lieutenant Robert Sharp's platoon to cover it. A Company, meanwhile, passed across the front of HQ Company to take up a position west of them. Sharp wrote afterwards:

May 24 Arrived at Ostricourt 0500 hrs. Stayed morning in new school room. About 1000 hrs down on truck to Carvin to find route. Back in truck and acted as guide to Lt Ellis bringing company on foot. Returned [through] wood north of road. Met OC Coy and across road, across field and down to river about 1400 hrs. Bridges had been blown. Men fed at haystack. Orders that enemy were expected soon. Position partially pre-pared. At about 1730 hrs moved up river about 500 yards, nearly to next bridge east, and dug positions. Large slag heaps on opposite bank. Had barges sunk and fires on same put out. At dusk, about 2100 hrs reported to OC Coy that French soldiers were moving into my weapon pits and saw Lt Hugh Pope, with men, moving down bank to take up position. About 2200 hrs on to lorries & round to Pont Maudit. Received orders and prepared position with wreckage from blown bridge and sandbags. Moroccan troops there with two French officers. Quiet all night.[17]

Captain Brown in fact records that HQ Company's move was delayed, because one of the two company trucks was away at the regimental aid post, where two casualties from the company had been taken. The two soldiers had been wounded by a rifle going off, apparently accidentally, but Brown's comment upon this seems to imply that he believed the wounds might actually have been self-inflicted.

The battalion line now covered some 8 miles and ran in order from north-west to south-east: C Company, A Company, HQ Company, D Company. Language difficulties and mutual mistrust made Anglo-French co-operation difficult at any level during the 1940 campaign, but further problems arose on the ground because interspersed between the companies of the 2nd/5th Leicesters were French Senegalese and Moroccan colonial troops. In 1940 the

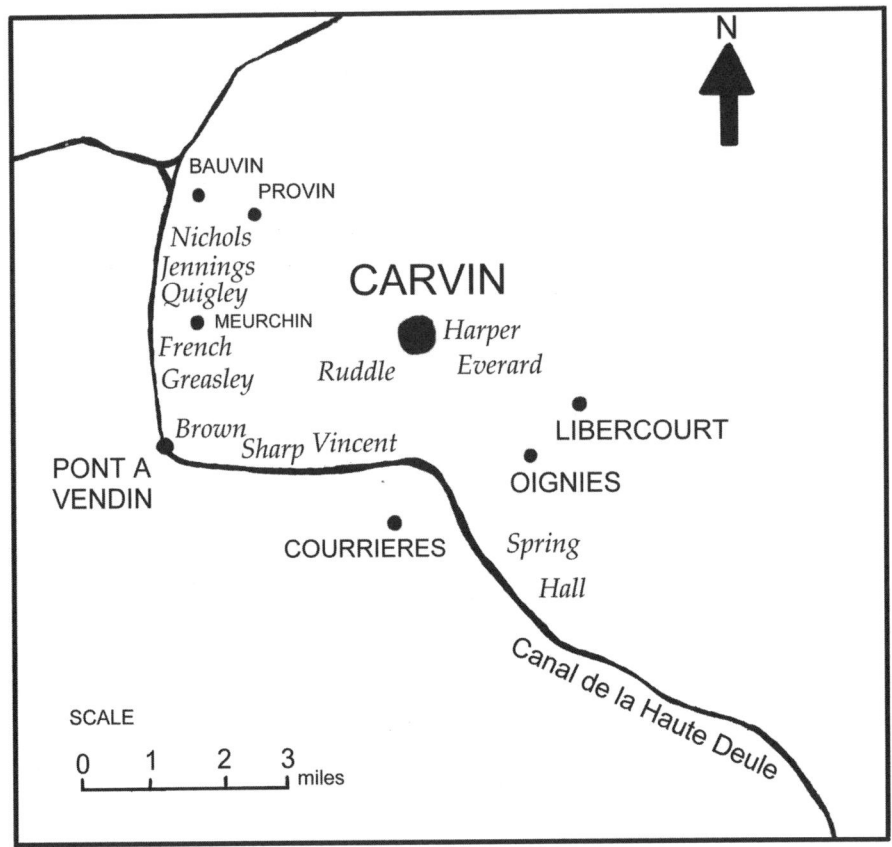

The relative locations of some of the soldiers mentioned in the text on 26 May 1940.

morale and effectiveness of the French Army as a whole was low, but the officers commanding these neighbouring colonial troops made it clear to the Leicesters from the outset that if a serious German attack was to develop, they did not expect their men to stand and fight. To be fair, colonial troops were ill–used by their metropolitan French commanders. Those on the canal bank must have been well aware that French generals on the Western Front in the First World War had gained a bad reputation for putting Senegalese soldiers into the first waves of any attack in preference to French troops, using them quite literally as cannon fodder. The Germans also seem to have treated the Senegalese more harshly than white French troops. There are a number of documented cases from the 1940 campaign of German troops shooting Senegalese captives whilst French soldiers were spared.

On Saturday 25 May an advanced battalion HQ was set up at Meurchin. Lieutenant Colonel Ruddle spent the day touring the forward positions, inspecting the defences and doing his best to encourage the men, chatting to them as they huddled in hastily dug slit trenches or taking what cover they could in buildings near the canal. From today's perspective, seventy years on, it is not always easy to appreciate how poorly prepared these men were for the operation with which they were tasked. Yet it is almost impossible for the writer to over emphasise how lacking in some of the most basic aspects of the soldier's craft they really were, and two examples are given to support this. At this time, about to face the enemy in the most serious engagement thus far in the history of the 2nd/5th Leicesters, Private Don French had never fired a rifle. He stated later on a number of occasions that, in spite of being called up in January of 1940, he did not actually fire a live round (or a round of any kind) until July 1945 when he returned to the Army from a POW camp. Private Victor Clough, meanwhile, recalled that on another occasion, whilst in France:

> One bloke came up to me – [with] the Lee-Enfield rifle, you flick the front of the bolt up, and you can pull the bolt out. Well somehow or other, he'd flicked this up, pulled his bolt back, and he came to me [with the bolt in his hand] and he says, 'Look, I've broken me rifle, what do I do?'!![18]

The 2nd/5th battalion was about to fight its first and only battle in France as a formation. Even if it were not so poorly disposed along too long a front, it would have been practically impossible for the commanding officer to fight a battalion battle. Once any attack started, it would become virtually impossible for the front-line companies to stay in contact with each other or, more importantly, with battalion HQ. Signals Officer Lieutenant Jack Townsend had come to France in April 1940 equipped with just 50yd of telephone cable and one telephone. When the battalion had reached Seclin, he had commandeered five extra motor bikes in order to run messages to and fro, but this was hardly adequate for the task in hand.

Poorly armed, with obsolete weapons they had had little chance to practise with, ammunition in short supply, no mortars to provide close artillery support and just a few Bren guns dispersed among them, as thunder clouds gathered overhead even the weather seemed to be against the Leicesters. There was little else the Tommies could do now but to try to find what shelter they could from the rain, either by pulling ground sheets over their slit trenches or by taking cover in farmhouses behind the front line, and await the coming onslaught.

Chapter 3

Battle and Retreat

Huddled in makeshift weapon pits in groups of seven or eight, or if they were lucky in billets in abandoned farmhouses, the men of the 2nd/5th Leicesters lined the northern bank of the Canal de la Haute Deule near Carvin and awaited the approach of the German armies from the south. An expendable rearguard, they would not have long to wait for an encounter with the enemy.

Most published accounts of the battle that was to follow place the crossing of the canal by the Germans on 26 May 1940. However, advanced German patrols seem to have crossed it on their own initiative on the previous afternoon. The most-detailed surviving account of the battle on the canal from the perspective of the 2nd/5th Leicesters comes from HQ Company, under the command of Captain Sidney Brown. Whilst in captivity he prepared a meticulous account of what happened that day:

> Coy sector was 1½ miles Pont de Maudit (Carvin–Lens Rd) inclusive to Pont Vendin Rly Bridge inclusive. Mr Sharp at Pont de Maudit, PSM Holtham E side of Rly Bridge at Esteville, Sgt Sales, W side of that Railway bridge & PSM Simpson at Vendin with Essex (?) Regt. Information given that French troops were other side of canal but we might expect odd German AFVs. Coy HQ moved to Esteville. French patrol returned with information that no French troops were other side of canal and German troops were advancing from Lens. Bn HQ advised, doubted information, & while there saw map that had been captured from Germans giving positions of advancing German troops. Saw centre of my sector was in for trouble, so hastily returned via Mr Sharp to Coy.
>
> Visited PSM Simpson & told Essex (?) Regt were withdrawing so had to hastily alter his positions. 1400 hrs [25 May] attack began in front of Coy HQ spreading west to Vendin & later starting on Eastern portion. Advised BN HQ & asked for more men. CO & Adjt arrived about 1600 hrs during a quiet period but were unable to get to front line. Promised to

send what help he could. Immediately attack started a lot of French came running back but about 1800 hrs more French arrived & tried to get to canal down railway embankment. Soon gave up. About 2000 hrs more French withdrew. About 2130 hrs set out with Coy HQ to attempt to reach PSM Holtham. Tried going down through spinney but undergrowth too thick. Tried again by side of spinney & got half way having struggled through two wire fences when I heard truck driver calling my name & saying Capt Gee had arrived. So all returned. Two sections had arrived each with a Bren Gun. As Mr Ellis had not returned I told Capt Gee what was happening & asked him to place one section as best as possible as it was dark to cover the blown railway bridge from the west side while I placed the one on the east side. Both sections started digging in and as Mr Ellis had still not returned I left CQMS Hughes in charge & set out with CSM Chambers to visit PSM Holtham. It was about 2300 hrs & pitch black, visibility being only about 2 yards. About halfway down I heard digging & as everything was quiet I imagined the remaining French had come back and were digging in there. We moved quietly towards them & did not realise that they were Germans, in fact not until I had spoken to them in French & they stood up. It was then too late to get

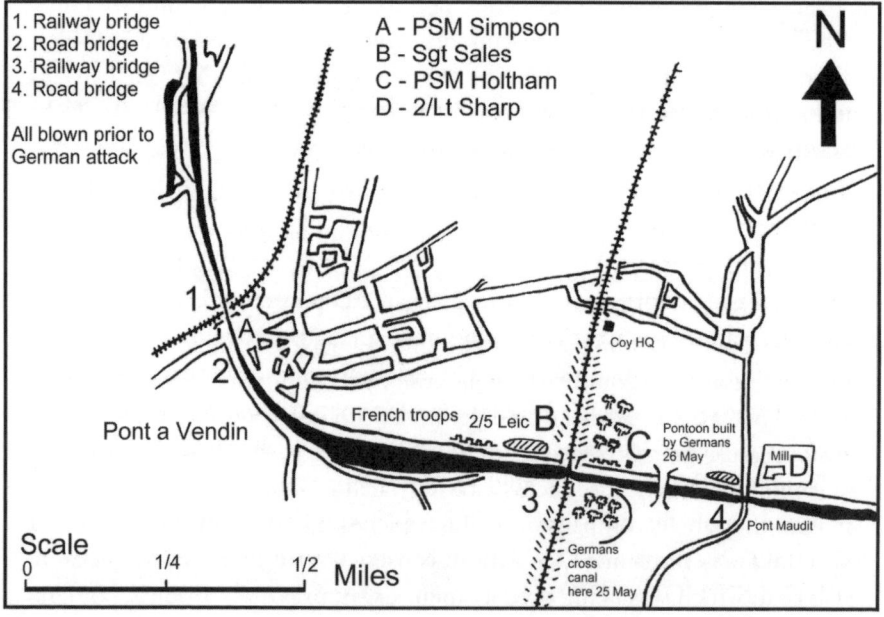

The detailed dispositions of HQ Company, 2nd/5th Leicesters, 25 and 26 May 1940.

back as they were all around us & we were both taken prisoners. The only thing I could do was let out a yell that Germans were there & hope that the section 100–150 yards behind us would hear. We spent the rest of the night lying on our backs, having been stripped of all equipment, near the canal. It rained most of the night and shells kept passing over our heads & falling near the old railway bridge.[1]

During the night of 25/26 May, enemy forces were observed further along the Leicesters' front, massing on the far side of the canal and screened in places by woodland. In fact the enemy had arrived in considerable strength now. Several German divisions were lined up facing the Canal Line along its entire length and awaiting the order to cross it. Opposing the men of the Leicestershire Regiment were assault troops from the leading elements of the German 12th Infantry Division. This division's recognition symbol was a bull pawing the ground in a menacing fashion, and its members were nearly all battle-hardened veterans of the 1939 Poland campaign. In contrast to the enfeebled British 46th Division, the German division fielded three infantry regiments, an artillery regiment, reconnaissance battalion, anti-tank battalion, engineer battalion and signal battalion.

During the hours of darkness, as their officers had predicted, at least some of the French colonial infantry also holding the canal defences withdrew. This left the individual companies of the 2nd/5th even more isolated than before, and without a continuous line of defence it was now inevitable that German forces would cross the canal at the weakest points, and envelop them. Richard Everard, with B Company in Carvin, recorded:

We spent an uneventful night and next day, 25 May, various patrols were sent out round the outskirts of Carvin. We moved the Company into a small outhouse and an old chapel. That night 'B' Company was still in reserve, and some men were sent to reinforce 'HQ' Company, who, with cooks etc. were holding part of the line. During the night our artillery was very active, we could hear shells going over all night and we thought it was grand, as we had been told Jerry had no guns, only light cycle and armoured car patrols. Once again how wrong we were! Because early next morning, 26 May, the enemy started shelling the town. Geoff [Gee] moved the whole company into slit trenches by the colliery, which had been made by the miners for ARP purposes. We were very close to a large slag heap which was being used as an observation post by French gunners. There were a lot of Jerry planes about … about 10.00am we saw nearly thirty Stukas circling round. Then they peeled off one by one and dived on the observation post. We could see the bombs coming out. I was reading Adrian Bell's *Cherry Tree*; there was nothing we could do about the bombing but hope for the best. Bombs were dropping all around us, accompanied that horrible screeching peculiar to the Stuka ... a colliery building close to us had a direct hit; everyone was covered in brick and coal dust and worse still, our two company trucks were buried under the debris of the building.[2]

Private 'Moe' Harper was also in B Company and remembered: '[At] Carvin we set up around the mines (coal). We were again heavily Stuka'd and shelled by Boche artillery. When the time came to withdraw again we all looked more like Kentucky minstrels than troops, we were covered in coal dust.'[3]

Captain Sidney Brown, already a German captive, had a grandstand view of the battle from the German lines as it unfolded:

May 26th At dawn I saw that about a whole Bn was over the canal. They already had two wireless sets working & also field telephone working. Two of their 4½″ mortars were working just near me & I watched them lobbing them down near where I had left Coy HQ, but could see none of our men. Later in the day we were moved to Esteville & on the way I saw no sign of my men or the trucks & realised that they must have moved out. No food at all, slept in barn.[4]

Captain Brown's family had no news of him until 21 June 1940, when they received a postcard from him stating that he was a prisoner of war but was in good health. Also captured in the fighting on the canal was his batman, Private Thomas Wilcox. However, it was to be July 1940 before his wife, whom he had just recently married and who lived at Warrington Street in Leicester, received the news that he too was safe.

Lieutenant Robert Sharp, as already noted, was holding the Pont Maudit, about half a mile east of Pont a Vendin, and about a quarter of a mile further along the canal from the position at which Captain Brown was captured. This was roughly the centre of the Leicesters' line on 26 May 1940. Today the Pont Maudit has been replaced by a modern road bridge carrying the D917 between Lille and Lens, however satellite imagery reveals that the footings for the original 1940 bridge still exist. Sharp has left a detailed account of what happened there, further adding to what is known of HQ Company's movements that day:

25th May CO came and I received orders to stay there from him. Set troops out as on plan. Firing started down river to west about 1400 hrs. Troops good. Rain at night and mortars. Helped for about 20 minutes by light RA (unknown). Lt Ellis came with ammunition about 2300 hrs. Sent two runners to Coy HQ. Results unknown. Did not return.

May 26th Fighting at fairly short range through out morning, and found enemy getting through down on right. At about 1300 hrs enemy artillery ranged on bridge perfectly, killed a few French, & stayed there. Drew men back from that side into yard. French Captain Thurbin then took command, and said we would hold & go south that night. French on east of position gave way & enemy came through & swarmed into yard at about 1530 hrs, 26th May 40. Orders from French captain to surrender.[5]

Corporal Dick Vincent was a section commander in Robert Sharp's platoon. He and his men were holding a position in a corn mill overlooking the road bridge over the Deule Canal, at Pont Maudit. He clearly remembered many years later that during the afternoon of 25 May a French officer from a neighbouring unit had come across with four or five of his soldiers and told the Leicesters there that once the German attack began, after dark they would be able to slip across the bridge, through the German lines and away to safety. However, when the German attack started in earnest early the following morning the position was overwhelmed before anyone could have a chance to escape, and the French officer very quickly raised the white flag. Vincent wrote later:

I remember the Germans taking us prisoners across the canal by boat, it was pulled across by rope. We then went to a farm where there were other prisoners – French Senegalese and Moroccans – in a small area, and a machine gun mounted to keep us in . . . that night a few, say about twenty POWs were put into a hayloft to sleep – the best nights sleep for over a week! At some point we were given some cooked macaroni. We got to Arras to be placed in to what I think was a barracks along with plenty of other British POWs. Here I met up with my Second Lieutenant, R. Sharp. Where he had been up to then I had no idea, perhaps the Germans had separated the officers from us.[6]

George Arlott was also in HQ Company and remembered:

We were dug in alongside a canal. On the left hand side. When the Germans came down, I always remember, it was a Sunday morning, very misty with fog, and you could see these figures, moving about, moving about in the distance, and we were told they were Germans ... We had one rifle, fifteen rounds per man. Against the might of the German army! It was in bandoliers round your neck, that's how you carried it ... We weren't roughed up, nothing like that. We were treated well, as well as you can expect from a victorious army ... As far as I can remember, we were in a barn and behind bales of straw, and there was a bloody great German appeared at the barn door, well he appeared big to me, because I'd only just woke up you see, been asleep ... He said, 'hande hoch' which we took to mean 'hands up' and our sergeant, he said, 'Never, you bastards', he shouted, but this jerry, he had a hand grenade in his hand, a stick grenade, this was in the barn door ... he threatened him with it. And when he threatened him the sergeant must have put his rifle down ... [then we were] lined up outside, and I thought we were all going to be shot! But they took us across the canal, they'd got these boats on the canal, rubber boats which they pulled across with ropes ... and they marched us to a village, where we were put in a square, and the Germans had these machine guns on tripods, and they were aimed at the wall and the wall was marked with these bullet marks where they'd obviously shot people, [so] I was a bit concerned! And this German officer came, from nowhere, and started talking to us, and tried to get us talking, to say who we were with. He started off by saying, 'We know more about you than you know yourself, for instance, you belong to the 2nd/5th Leicesters' ... there seemed to be respect between their officers [and ours]. Various saluting went on.[7]

Arlott remembered that in spite of the relatively civilised treatment he and his comrades received from their captors, food was not forthcoming. This may have been simply due to the fact that the Germans were advancing beyond their supply lines, but it was also a well-known German practice to deprive prisoners of food in the early stages of captivity, when they were most likely to try to try to overpower their guards or escape, in order to induce fatigue and lethargy.

As the morning wore on, those portions of HQ Company still holding out against the Germans came under intense pressure. Sustained machine-gun and mortar fire was directed at them and among those hit was Second Lieutenant Hugh Pope. His men tried to carry him back to a place of safety but it was too late, he was severely wounded and died almost at once. Pope had joined the battalion in January 1940 from the Royal Military College at Sandhurst. He was one of the brightest young officers in the battalion. Prior to Sandhurst he had been studying theology at Lincoln, after graduating from Sidney Sussex College, Cambridge. Before that he had been at Oakham School, where he had captained the cricket XI. As a young subaltern, he had showed enormous potential, on one occasion being congratulated by the divisional commander during an exercise at Bradgate Park, for the efficient and confident manner in which he gave his orders. His obituary in the regimental magazine the *Green Tiger* read: 'He showed great promise as a young Platoon Commander ... and he might well have gone far. But it was not to be.'[8]

Hugh Pope was aged 22 when he died, and today he lies in Carvin Communal Cemetery. Further away, to the north of the battalion sector, C Company was also in a desperate fight. Here, another young officer and platoon commander was to die that day. Second Lieutenant John Emerton, like Hugh Pope, had attended Oakham School. In 1939 after leaving school, he had joined the ranks of the 5th battalion Leicestershire Regiment. With the outbreak of war he applied for a commission, and after time at an Officer Cadet Training Unit he was commissioned and posted back to the 2nd/5th battalion. His obituary in the *Green Tiger* read:

> He was a most enthusiastic young platoon officer and extremely popular with all ranks. His quiet but cheerful disposition and his growing efficiency held out great hopes for the future ... During the action [in which he died] he showed the finest qualities of leadership and did much to encourage his men when they were greatly outnumbered both in personnel and weapons.[9]

Emerton was aged only 20 when he died. His body was not recovered and today he is commemorated on the panels of the Dunkirk Memorial to the Missing. One of his section commanders, Corporal Andrew Quigley, was killed along-side him. Quigley was a Regular NCO who had returned from India to join the battalion. Emerton and Quigley were operating one of the company's few Bren guns in a forward and exposed position when they were hit. One of the survivors of C Company recalled, many years later, as he withdrew seeing the corporal slumped lifeless over the gun, his helmet slipped down over his face. Quigley was aged 26, and left a widow at Lutterworth. For his bravery in the fighting of that day, by which in spite of the danger to himself he inspired other men to stay at their posts, he was awarded a posthumous Mention in

Despatches. Quigley's bravery was also remembered many years later by one of the members of his section, a frightened young conscript from South Wigston by the name of Private Alf Nichols. The calmness of his more-experienced section commander, in the face of heavy enemy fire, had clearly made a deep impression upon Nichols. Quigley, like Emerton the equally gallant young officer who died with him, is commemorated on the Dunkirk Memorial to the Missing.

The situation now was desperate and although men sold their lives dearly, it was hopeless to continue. Most of the forward troops were now effectively surrounded. Private Maurice Jennings who was there with C Company remembered:

> We were billeted in a house on the canal [overlooking] a road bridge. There were only nine of us [in my section] and the corporal and lance corporal went off with the Bren Gun [and] left seven of us on our own, nobody in charge, all of us frightened. So I left out the back [door] as there was a cornfield to try and make contact with somebody. [I] only had a rifle and five rounds. I used the field for cover but I was shot in my left hand and captured [by the Germans]. There were two of them, they cut my webbing and marched me with a gun in my back to the canal side and pushed me into a boat to the other side, then marched me into a farm yard where there were others and stood me up against a wall. [They had] a machine gun, we with our hands above our heads, we thought they were going to shoot us all. [After this] we were split up.[10]

Those members of C Company who had held their positions were now overrun. These men were marched away across the fields, hands above their heads, into captivity. As the situation deteriorated, the remainder of the company had begun to withdraw, under the command of the most senior NCO, the Company Sergeant Major, Andrew Croxall.

Rumours of what was taking place on the canal bank were now beginning to filter back to battalion headquarters, though there was no clear information. The commanding officer, Lieutenant Colonel Kenneth Ruddle, prepared a detailed account of his own movements, shortly after the battle. Under 26 May he recorded:

> Went to Bn HQ at BUQUEUX – found no messages there either from Bde or from Coys. Very soon we were severely shelled and then dive bombers attacked us for over two hours. At the end of this there were no

Major Guy German, the 2nd/5th battalion's first commanding officer. (*Mrs J. Haywood*)

Company Sergeant Major Arthur Chambers, of 75 Owen Street, Coalville, a miner in civil life and a pre-war Territorial soldier. (*Mr J. Chambers*)

Lance Corporal Dick Vincent, one of the first recruits for the 2nd/5th battalion. (*Mr R. Vincent*)

Number 7 platoon, A Company, at the 2nd/5th battalion's only camp, Holyhead, summer 1939. Back row, left to right: Shenton, Hazelden, Lucas, unknown, Newbrokes, unknown, Allot, Hertsorn, Witherington; middle row: Parker, Hunt, Healey, Buswell, Smith, Crease, Robinson, Bates; front row: Bickle, Corporal Vincent, Sergeant Shingler, Lance Corporal Matts. (*Mr R. Vincent*)

Second Lieutenant Jack Townsend and his platoon march past a saluting base at the Holyhead camp, 1939. (*Mr J. Townsend*)

Sergeant F.T.E. Snow. He had joined the Army in 1931, and upon his return from India he was posted to the 2nd/5th battalion. (*Mr M.C. Smith*)

Major Kenneth Ruddle, who succeeded Guy German as commanding officer of the 2nd/5th battalion. (*Trustees of the Royal Leicestershire Regiment*)

Major Ken Symington, who had a long association with the 5th Leicesters. He became second-in-command of the 2nd/5th battalion, and commanded the remains of the battalion on the retreat to Dunkirk. (*Trustees of the Royal Leicestershire Regiment*)

Private George Arlott, a process engraver in the printing trade. He enlisted in October 1939, and was captured on 26 May 1940. (*Mr G. Arlott*)

Officers of the 2nd/5th battalion in Leicester, early 1940. Left to right: Doc Rankin (MO), Captain Geoffrey Gee, unknown, Lieutenant and Quartermaster Tom Hall, Second Lieutenant Robert Sharp (POW 26 May 1940), unknown, Second Lieutenant Charlie Hughes (Transport Officer, KIA 26 May 1940), Captain Sidney Brown (POW 26 May 1940), unknown, Captain Mike Moore, unknown. (*Mrs M. Moore*)

Private Joseph Kynoch, who served initially with the 2nd/5th battalion before transfer to the 1st/5th. (*Mr J. Kynoch*)

Lieutenant R.F.J. O'Reilly. A Regular officer, he returned from India to join the 2nd/5th battalion. He was taken prisoner on 26 May 1940 near Carvin. (*Author's collection*)

Second Lieutenant Eric Capron. A Grimsby trawler owner, he was commissioned in 1940. He was evacuated from France via Dunkirk but was later killed in action in Italy. (*Major P. Moore*)

A French postcard sent home by Private Victor Clough, spring 1940. (*Mr V. Clough*)

A section of the 2nd/5th battalion photographed outside their billets, on Eastern Boulevard, Leicester, spring 1940. (*Mr G. Nichols*)

Lieutenant J.W.B. Marshall, a Regular officer who joined the 2nd/5th battalion as Adjutant whilst in France. He was badly injured in a motor-cycle accident on 26 May 1940. (*Trustees of the Royal Leicestershire Regiment*)

Regimental Sergeant Major Edwin Ross DCM. When the fighting began in May 1940 he ordered his men to throw their cap badges down a well. (*Major A.E.R. Ross*)

The factory of Métallurgie Lilloise, Lesquin, used as a billet by the 2nd/5th battalion on the way to the front on 19 May 1940. (*Author's collection*)

LESQUIN (Nord) — La Métallurgie lilloise

Lieutenant Cliff Marriott. On 21 May he was left behind at Emmerin to supervise the kit when the 2nd/5th battalion went into action. (*Major P. Moore*)

Private H.J. Collins, HQ Company, of Fairfield Road, Market Harborough. On 23 May he was sent by Captain Brown to forage for milk on a farm, but returned empty-handed after being fired upon by French soldiers. (*Mr H.J. Collins*)

The railway bridge over the Deule Canal at Courrières, defended in May 1940 by the 2nd/5th Leicesters. By this time the bridge had been demolished by French engineers. The coal barges were also sunk so as not to provide cover for the enemy. (*Author's collection*)

Mine buildings at Carvin, where B Company waited in reserve as the attack unfolded on 26 May 1940. (*Author's collection*)

Private J.L. 'Moe' Harper, of Leicester, who was with B Company at Carvin, and who took shelter in the coal yard. He remembered, 'We looked more like Kentucky minstrels than soldiers'. (*Mr J.L. Harper*)

Platoon Sergeant Major T.F. Simpson, of HQ company. He and his men held the remains of the road bridge at Pont a Vendin until they were captured. (*Mr R. Vincent*)

The road bridge over the Deule Canal at Pont a Vendin. This bridge, which had by then been blown up, was at the centre of the 2nd/5th Leicesters' line on 26 May 1940. A group of HQ Company under Platoon Sergeant Major T.F. Simpson held positions on the far bank. (*Author's collection*)

serious casualties – only a few minor wounds and some shell shock cases. DRs and others who had been trying to get through to Coys brought rumours that the enemy had broken through and crossed the canal in various places, but no message from Coys, so tried again to get in touch with Coys. Owing to lack of DRs, long distances, and continual shellfire and bombing this proved impossible. The adjutant then went on motor-cycle to try and contact 'A' Coy but came back having had a bad crash – very shaken with damaged jaw and bleeding face etc. Later he was evacuated to LILLE hospital.[11]

In fact the Adjutant, Lieutenant Marshall, was destined to play no further part in his battalion's battle as a consequence of the motor-cycle crash – no doubt due to the rain-soaked roads following a night of thunderstorms – which resulted in a broken jaw and several lost teeth. He was taken from hospital directly to Dunkirk.

Meanwhile, A Company was holding positions northwards from Pont a Vendin railway bridge, which had already been destroyed. Their positions were in more-open country, amid fields of swaying corn and in part covered a small bridge carrying a local road between the farms on opposite sides of the canal. The canal at this point is today crossed by the modern suspended road bridge, carrying the carriageway of the D165 main road across the water towards Carvin. But in 1940 a much smaller structure crossed the canal here at a more acute angle, serving the cart tracks which can still just be discerned on satellite imagery of the location today.

Early on the morning of 26 May, the attack on this position began to develop in earnest. Some members of A Company, including Private Horace 'Jim' Greasley, had been stood down and were still asleep in a farm about a hundred yards back from the Canal Line when the German attack erupted out of a grey dawn. The chatter of machine guns and the heavy thud of mortar rounds awoke Greasley and his comrades, and they ran to take up positions in the hastily dug slit trenches overlooking the canal. The bridge here, a narrow stone-built structure about wide enough for a truck, had not yet been destroyed and a German advanced guard was seen approaching through the cornfield beyond. Possibly believing that they would encounter no resistance, these men began to cross. They were all killed by a volley of fire from the platoon Bren gun, and some of Greasley's platoon ran forward to check that they were dead.

However the swaying corn in front of them was now alive with figures in field-grey, as more Germans began moving up to take the place of those who had been killed. Even more of the enemy were working their way behind the isolated A Company positions, through the yawning gaps in the line created by the French withdrawal during the night. Outflanked, Greasley's platoon was soon forced to surrender. He remembered their German captors looking for any information relating to their unit:

> The men [in my section] weren't really roughed up at that time [by the Germans], [but] they were all searched and made to turn their battledress uniform pockets inside out. They had to drop their pouches (webbing) on the ground, and walk about a hundred yards away from it. We had no personal papers on us, though I managed to conceal a nail file.[12]

Further away but still with A Company, as enemy mortar and machine-gun fire tore up the ground around him, Private Don French was sent back by his platoon sergeant to company headquarters to ask for instructions as to what to do. He could find no one who could help, as the company was in disarray and headquarters staff were already falling back. He returned to the front-line positions and his comrades to find that the Germans had worked their way along the canal from a crossing point further along, and had got around behind them. In addition to the Germans advancing across the fields in front of them, they were now taking heavy fire from the rear, and the position was becoming hopeless. Some Tigers tried to make their way back across the fields towards where company HQ had been, but were picked up by Germans as they did so. French himself was in no position to flee, as by this time he had been hit in the left shoulder by a machine-gun bullet and was bleeding heavily. He reminisced ruefully years later that if he had not returned to the front line, but had simply kept going, he would not have been captured.

Despite having been issued with only twenty-five rounds of ammunition, some men still had twenty or so left on them when captured. Instructions to use it sparingly were taken too literally by some. Some of the men who were too slow to lay down their weapons were roughly treated by the Germans, who felled them with rifle butts. French remembered: 'I saw one or two get a bloody good hiding off the Jerries. Two or three of them set about one chap, making him holler and shout ... because he wouldn't put down his rifle.'[13] He remained bitter for the rest of his life that he had not seen a single officer during that whole period on the canal bank, but the fact remains that officers <u>were</u> in the front line with their men – several of them were killed that day, after all.

It is generally agreed that the most dangerous time for a prisoner of war is not in the long years spent in POW camps, but in the hours and minutes directly after capture, when the blood of the enemy is still up. This is the time when the out-of-hand murder of POWs is most likely to occur. A number of atrocities occurred in the 1940 campaign, for example the murder of a party of the Royal Warwickshire Regiment by their captors at Wormhoudt, or the incident in which a group of soldiers from the Royal Norfolk Regiment was shot by German troops at Le Paradis. However, there is no evidence to suggest that any of the fatal casualties sustained by the Leicesters were killed in cold blood, and most of those taken prisoners seem to have been reasonably well treated by their captors.

At the extreme south-east of the 2nd/5th Leicesters' line stood D Company, holding positions south of the suburb of Oignies. Among them was Private Gordon Spring, one of the D Company men who escaped the debacle. Spring remembered:

We were ... digging in, going to defend a canal. I said to myself: 'Bloody Hell Gordon, you are going to fight for your country.' We were armed with rifles, one Bren Gun per 100 men and grenades.

I was at one end with the Bren Gun and an anti-tank rifle and we could see the German Panzers approaching and preparing to attack in a fork movement. We heard that the Jerries had crossed the canal. I was sent to collect ammo and on my return, I found that the Germans had crossed the canal near us and killed all the lads. I was then on my own.

This was my baptism of fire. Imagine my stunned disbelief at what I saw. Mates, alive a few minutes ago, now lying dead, their gaping wounds making me feel sick and the growing panic of the realisation that I was by myself, maybe surrounded by God knows what. This was only the beginning of my hell at Dunkirk.[14]

Gordon also witnessed one of his boyhood friends from Hinckley, Private Joseph Gamble, blown up by the blast of a shell. Gamble, the son of Mr and Mrs Gamble of 27 Westfield Road, Hinckley, has no known grave and today is commemorated on the Dunkirk Memorial to the Missing.

Private Jim Hall of Burbage was also there with D Company. He remembered:

We were put in a defensive position on a river or canal, and near us were some railway sidings. The bridge across the canal had been blown. It was just sagging in the middle. It was here that I saw my first Germans. I was platoon runner at the time so when the Sergeant went on a recce he took me with him. The Germans were on the other side of the canal amongst some factory buildings and we were on top of a railway embankment when I saw them.

I remember I started jumping up and down like a bloody two year old, pointing them out to my Sergeant and shouting, 'Germans'! The next thing I knew he had pushed me down the embankment saying, 'Get down you silly bugger!' We were there for about twenty-four hours [in total], mortar bombed and shelled etc., and then we got ordered to get out. We needed no second telling. We did![15]

As the day progressed, battalion HQ had moved to the north side of Carvin, in order to seek respite from the shelling which had been continuous almost all day. Richard Everard, meanwhile, was caught up in the chaos as control of the battle slipped away from Lieutenant Colonel Ruddle and his officers. With such an extended position to hold and with such poor communications, it would have been hard to fight an effective battalion battle even if they had not been hit by a blitzkrieg of shelling and air attacks. Everard describes the situation:

We moved from the slit trenches across the railway lines to battalion HQ. There was confusion there. The Company became divided, half with Geoff and me and the rest with Eric Capron and Company Sergeant Major Monty Burton. We received orders from the CO to withdraw across country. In this confusion and chaos I saw Lieutenant Charlie Hughes and Lieutenant Botibol, and it was the last time I ever did see them. They were killed within the next few days. They were both grand fellows.[16]

Ruddle continues his account thus:

There were rumours at this stage that various Coys were withdrawing but nothing definite. Eventually I decided to move Bn HQ and reserve Coy a mile or so to a healthier position (i.e. further from artillery which was continually being attacked near our HQ). I hoped it would be easier to get in touch with Coys from a new position. (Soon after we left, a shell went through our vacated battalion HQ). All personnel under the 2nd i/c [Major Symington] and OC 'B' Coy [Captain Gee] moved across country. I went round by car with M.T.O. [Second Lieutenant Hughes] and the

QM [Lieutenant Hall] and on reaching CARVIN–CAMPHIN road I found a large number of troops – mostly DLIs [Durham Light Infantry] and some but not all of our Bn HQ and reserve Coy. (The remainder including the 2nd i/c, OC 'B' Coy, RSM etc. could not be traced and had apparently got separated from the others in the general congestion.)

At this moment the Divisional commander appeared and announced that he had got some French tanks to lead a counter attack. The DLIs were to send Coys along three separate routes to the canal. I managed to muster forty to fifty men who were attached to 'A' Coy DLI. I myself after seeing the troops march off, went to CARVIN by car with the IO [Lieutenant Botibol], followed by our other transport and the QM. I set up a Bn HQ on the north side of the town. The IO and I then set off to meet our troops who were advancing with the DLIs to the west of CARVIN. As we were moving out of the village a shell burst within a few yards of us and the IO was very severely wounded in the stomach. I had an ambulance down the road and so was able to get help within two or three minutes. He was taken off by ambulance.[17]

Even though it was possible to get medical attention to him almost immediately, Botibol's condition was critical after he was wounded by shell fragments. Although he was seen about an hour later passing in an ambulance through brigade headquarters, he was not heard of again for some months. It was hoped against hope by his fellow officers that he might somehow have been taken prisoner and survived, but eventually the news came from a French officer that he had, in the chaos and confusion, been taken to a French hospital outside Dunkirk. Botibol had died of his wounds two days after being injured, on 28 May 1940. The French officer contacted the officers of the 2nd/5th battalion and handed over his letters and personal papers, and passed on the information that he had been buried at Malo-les-Bains with full military honours in the presence of a number of French officers. Today Botibol's grave may still be seen in Malo-les-Bains Communal Cemetery, marked both with the tiger of the Leicestershire Regiment and the Star of David.

As the few men with him were attached pro tem to the 8th battalion Durham Light Infantry, Colonel Ruddle, meanwhile, was forced to defer to the commanding officer of that formation. He became a spectator as a wrangle broke out between the brigade commander, Durham Light Infantry officers and the local French commander, who refused to supply tanks for the planned counteroffensive. Without this support the Durhams would not attack, and contented themselves with attempting to defend Carvin against a further German advance.

Toward the end of the day on 26 May, and in the absence of any other means of communication, a patrol was sent out from battalion headquarters towards Pont a Vendin. This patrol was ordered to try to establish whether anyone from the forward companies of the 2nd/5th Leicesters was still holding their ground, and if they had not already been overrun, to pass on the message that they were to withdraw immediately. Even though it was not his main role, the battalion Transport Officer, Second Lieutenant Charlie Hughes, immediately volunteered to lead this patrol, in spite of being under heavy bombardment and without food all day. His obituary in the *Green Tiger* read:

> Owing to his cheerfulness and high spirits he found no difficulty in getting twenty other ranks to go with him. The patrol had not gone far when they ran into a most intense artillery barrage, and he and four of his men were killed outright. Fortunately he did not have to suffer, but his well known cheery smile and good companionship will be missed by his fellow officers and men.[18]

Charlie Hughes had lost his father in the First World War, and shortly after arriving in France himself, confided in another officer that he did not believe he would ever see England again either. He was, however, completely sanguine about this, and not in any way depressed by the thought. For his actions on 26 May 1940, Hughes received the award of a posthumous Mention in Despatches. His body was never recovered. Among the party who went with him was one of the transport sergeants, Shirley Pollard, in civilian life a boot and shoe-factory manager from Anstey. He too was Mentioned in Despatches for this action. Private Victor Clough was also a member of this patrol and remembered:

> Second Lieutenant Hughes was killed, I was only just down the road from him. He was our transport officer. I was in the transport section and he was our officer. He was killed when a shell burst among us. There was a Lance Corporal Hughes killed there as well. In those days they were all local men, there were none from outside.[19]

Lance Corporal Kenneth William Hughes, of Anstey, lies today in Carvin Communal Cemetery. He was aged 19 when he died. In the same incident, Private F. Woodward showed great bravery which was to earn him the Military

Medal, the only one awarded to the 2nd/5th battalion for the Dunkirk campaign. The citation read:

> Pte Woodward went out on patrol with an officer [Second Lieutenant Charlie Hughes] and twenty other ranks on the evening of 26th May at Carvin. All had been under fire nearly all day. He, however, showed great courage and cheerfulness and did much to keep up the spirits of the others. When his officer and four other ranks fell he attempted to get to them to help the wounded. The fire at that time made this impossible but after returning to Battalion Headquarters he immediately volunteered to go out with another party and fetch in the wounded. This he did, but all had been killed.[20]

For those remaining in the forward positions on the canal, things were now hopeless. Lieutenant O'Reilly was captured there, as was Lieutenant David White, also Private Walter Graves of Chester Street, Leicester, a former employee of the Grosvena Shoe Works. He had been wounded under the left arm by a mortar bomb fragment and was receiving treatment in an advanced dressing station when it was overrun. Medics and patients alike were captured. Privates Percy Smith and George Bottrell were wounded and captured, and were subsequently treated by the Germans at Ghent hospital. Lance Corporal Harold Frost was not so fortunate. He died of his wounds whilst in German hands before he could be evacuated, and was buried alongside many of his comrades in Carvin Communal Cemetery. Private Freddie Diaper of Leicester was also killed in action, and today has no known grave, being commemorated on the Dunkirk Memorial. He left a young widow, Nellie, in Leicester. The two had been married only a few months. A degree of mystery surrounds the death of Corporal William Francis, of Barwell. He lies today in Vendin le Vieil Communal Cemetery, on the German side of the canal. His is the only British grave in the village cemetery and the Commonwealth War Graves Commission records the date of his death as being between 27 and 31 May 1940. The likelihood seems to be that he was wounded when captured and subsequently died of his injuries, though the possibility cannot be ruled out that he was shot whilst in German hands.

Other men who went 'into the bag' there, were Sergeant C. Thompstone, of Captain Brown's HQ Company, a former employee of St Margaret's Flour Mills and a well-known member of Kibworth Golf Club; Private Phil Haywood, an engineer in civilian life and a member of the battalion band; Private Kenneth Callaghan, a hosiery hand from Leicester; Private Teddy Black of

Syston, a keen footballer who played for Syston St Peter's football team at left back; and Private Bob Monk of Market Harborough, the son of a Regular Army sergeant of the Leicesters. Lance Corporal Leonard Bingley and Private Raymond Whyatt, both of Leicester, were captured. Private Joe White, one of the battalion Bren gunners, was captured near the canal at Pont a Vendin. He and the fifteen or so men with him were quickly overwhelmed when the German attack erupted. White was disarmed by a Volkesdeutscher, an American-German who had returned to Germany in response to Hitler's call for her children to come to her aid when war broke out. It was a bizarre experience – the phrase has gone down as a movie cliché, but the German soldier really did say, 'For you Tommy, the war is over', albeit with a strong American accent. However, White did not have a chance to dwell on this for too long, as he and his comrades were now put in the terrifying position of being lined up in front of a machine gun – the Germans apparently intending to shoot them all in cold blood. Long minutes ticked by before it became apparent this was simply a tactic used to soften the prisoners up before interrogation.

For those who had managed to escape from the debacle on the Deule Canal, danger still lay ahead. The battalion had now begun to fragment and small parties battled their way to the coast as best they could. Sergeant Ian Noble and his section had been dug in, in slit trenches overlooking the canal on the morning of 26 May. As the early morning sun burnt off the mist, Noble had observed what he remembered many years later as 'grey things dragging black things towards the water'! To his astonishment he realised that these were German assault troops hauling rubber dinghies. With growing apprehension, his men asked Noble what they should do. Realising that another section of men who were on the far side of the canal were already beyond help, he pointed to a nearby vehicle and answered them succinctly, 'We're going to get in that truck and f*** off as fast as we can.' For the next week he was to shepherd his section through the chaos of the retreat, in the truck to begin with and when the fuel ran out, on foot. He was to arrive at Dunkirk having lost only one of his men to enemy action, sadly the youngest aged just 18.[21]

Lieutenant Richard Everard, Geoff Gee and Ken Symington were now withdrawing across country with about half of B Company. Everard remembered:

> There was a good deal of air burst shelling but we did not have any casualties. We went about three miles and then rested. We argued a bit as to exactly where we were. Doc Rankin and part of Battalion HQ had

joined us. By now it was dusk and we moved into Seclin – a town we had come through a little over fourteen days before in a very different mood. It was here that we had left our band instruments and the surplus baggage that had been brought up from Brittany. Most of the town was burning now. We all squeezed into one house – about forty other ranks (ORs), Ken Symington, Geoff Gee, Doc Rankin and myself. We stayed there till about 4.00am then moved out in the dark to get into cover and away from the town before it was light. We had learned by now that towns were unhealthy places in the daytime.

It was now 27 May. We found a convenient farmhouse, with an orchard and got everyone under cover. Ken and Geoff decided to go off and try to find Brigade HQ and get some information and orders, since we had had neither for the last twenty-four hours. There were too many French soldiers about for my liking who would not keep under cover. So after a 'recce' with Doc we moved farther down the road to another farm with more cover and no French. Later in the afternoon Geoff returned. Ken (Symington) had stayed with Brigade HQ who were unable to do anything for us, or give us any worthwhile information. They apparently thought our plight was pretty hopeless. Geoff had had, to put it mildly, a trying day, with a lot of bombing thrown in for good measure. The cooks were now preparing an evening meal. There had been much slaughter amongst the poultry, and one of the men, Foulds of Woodhouse Eaves, had milked a cow. We all had a shave (though I was the only one left with a razor). We decided to stay the night where we were.[22]

However at about 2200 hours machine-gun fire was heard, very close at hand, and this group decided to move on. Reluctantly, they left a roasted pig from the farmyard simmering in a pot. Everard continues the story:

We thought we would make for Lille. We set off. The whole sky was red with the fires from burning towns. We seemed surrounded then. We had four miles to go before we struck the main road. We had our company truck with us – a box on pram wheels! – that was one idea we did borrow from the French. We met a French company on the march and had a talk with their officer, who seemed a nice fellow. We arrived in Lille about 3.00am. The city was completely deserted, so we carried on till we reached the river. We told the men to rest. We had marched about fifteen miles on pavé that night.[23]

Everard and Gee went off on their own to try to find out what was happening. They could find no one except for a few excited Frenchmen, who told them that Lille was surrounded and all was lost. Everard remembered:

> Geoff and I walked back through the silent, deserted streets We did not say much but we were both thinking the same thoughts. It was the first time we had felt dejected. We got back to where we had left the Company but there was no one there. My equipment had gone too, which I had left with RSM Ross. What next? It began to get light. Geoff and I were completely on our own now and all we had in the way of equipment was our tin hats and gas masks. We thought our gas masks were an unnecessary encumber-ance and very improperly discarded them. We walked along the river bank until we saw a bridge. We found an RE officer who said he had seen our lads and told them to get across as he was going to blow the bridge any moment. We decided we would wait and go along with him after he had blown the bridge. We had some food with his men. There was only a very small rearguard left to hold the line of the river; he advised us not to wait for him so we decided to go on and hope that we would pick up our men.[24]

Years later, Geoff Gee would tell his children that he was the 'last man out of Lille'. He and Richard Everard would afterwards present one another with silver tankards, inscribed with the date 28 May 1940, as a memento of this incident.

Gordon Spring was also on the road, though with a different group, and remembered:

> There was nothing I could do except leave my dead mates behind and make for God Knows Where in the hope of rejoining others of our battalion.
>
> So imagine the state I am in – growingly confused, desperate to save myself and frightened. I realised very quickly that with the advance of the Germans being so fast, I actually had to leg it pretty quickly. This is against all the rules and your inbred inclination as a soldier, but what was I to do? I had to look after myself – I was alone with terror building all around me.
>
> I walked back and fell in with a group of other soldiers. I tagged onto another unit of men walking in the same direction. An officer came up and told us he would lead us to the coast road. We walked for a few days with no food or anything to drink. We slept a little where we could – anywhere.

Suddenly a dispatch rider came up and said to us that our officer was leading us the wrong way. He was an impostor, a German, leading us to captivity. We shot the officer. Were we right or wrong? This is the state we had now reached. We were around Lille but managed to slip the net at 3.00 in the morning.[25]

A party led by C Company's Sergeant Major, Andrew Croxall, was not so fortunate, and having managed to escape from the slaughter on the canal, were taken prisoner the following day, 27 May, on the line of retreat at La Bassée. Even though Croxall, a 47-year-old veteran of the First World War, was wounded he was still subjected to brutal treatment from his German captors, being punched and kicked as they attempted to extract information from him regarding his unit. Private Gordon Chaplin of Sileby, who was well known in Leicester before the war as the trumpeter with the Embassy Dance Band, was with this group. He remembered later that he also was roughly treated by his German captors and in his debrief statement upon repatriation he commented: 'I was forced by a number of the enemy to tell of my Regt and its movements, of which they got only my regiment.'[26] Even this, of course, was more than Chaplin was obliged to reveal, which under the terms of the Geneva Convention on treatment of prisoners of war was limited to his name, date of birth, rank and number.

With the withdrawal of the Durham Light Infantry soldiers from Carvin on 27 May, Lieutenant Colonel Ruddle had resumed command of the fifty or so Leicesters still with him. Having no dispatch rider, he sent an officer in his personal car to try to find brigade HQ and to request further orders. The officer returned saying that brigade HQ had gone. At this point he received an out-of-date message ordering his withdrawal to Thumeries. Ruddle takes up the story once again:

As we were now many hours late for getting to the meeting point at THUMERIES, where according to the message buses would be waiting to withdraw the Bn to a resting place, I decided to take the party I had in our own transport to STEENVORDE by the route given. I had to give up the idea of locating the rest of the battalion, even if I had found them that would have made us even later still, and we would have had little chance of contacting the brigade at all. Eventually we did arrive at STEENVORDE at about midday, only to find another battle raging on the outskirts of the town and nobody knew anything about 139th brigade or 46th Div except that everyone who had come there had gone and we were advised to move on in the POPERINGHE direction.[27]

On the way to Steenvorde, Ruddle's party had stopped at Armentières to enquire the way. Whilst there, Captain Mike Moore of D Company was accidentally shot in the foot by a sergeant discharging his rifle in error. This unfortunate incident caused further delays as a passing ambulance was stopped and Moore was taken in it to hospital.

Private Jim Hall of Burbage and most of his company had managed to withdraw in reasonably good order from the canal bank. He recalled fifty years later:

> [We] saw a lot more of the French countryside as we got our usual quota of bombing etc. Marching here and marching there, I can't remember much about places or dates, but it was about this time when I lost contact with my Company.
>
> Later on two NCOs and myself with an officer, were told to take a load of barbed wire to a wood three or four miles away. Whilst unloading the wire a German spotter plane came over. We thought it was a Dutch plane and waved to him! The officer went back to the company telling us to wait in the wood till the main body of men arrived. It didn't! But we hadn't been in the wood long when three dive bombers plastered it. All that effort for just three of us and a pile of bloody barbed wire!
>
> By this time there was such chaos we were just wandering around, and after two or three days we came upon a Royal Engineers Bridging Company who were billeted in a large house. The area seemed to be alive with activity but one of the NCOs told me to see if I could scrounge some tea for them. They went up some steps into a large room and I went off and found what had been the cookhouse and made some tea. The cooks and everyone else were packing up, and the Engineers were blocking the road with their bridging equipment.
>
> Finally, after some time I got the tea and went back to the room where I had left them, only to find that they had vanished! I kept looking for them but no luck! The Engineers then arrived outside and kept shouting for me to come on, as the Germans were here! So I got on the lorry and went with them! Later on I found that the men I had gone to get the tea for had all been captured in that room whilst I was away getting it, and had spent four-and-a-half years in German prison camps. It was certainly my luckiest cup of tea![28]

The Engineers who had picked up Hall were under orders to make for Dunkirk, and their lorry began the winding journey through northern France, along roads strewn with the debris of war, towards the coast.

From a wider perspective, the position of the BEF and their French allies was now critical. The German attack on the Belgian Army in the north intensified, and the Belgians threatened to capitulate, forcing Gort to divert more troops to Belgium to try to hold the line around Ypres. If the Germans managed to break through to the Channel, they would have encircled the British and French armies with disastrous results. The French High Command proposed a joint Anglo-French counterattack to the south, but had by this stage utterly lost their grip on the reality of the situation. The planned attack to the south called upon French formations that had either been shattered in an encounter with the Germans already or whose morale had evaporated – in many cases both. The British High Command could see this, even if the French could not.

Gort, meanwhile, made the most important and far-reaching decision of his period in command of the BEF. He chose to disobey his orders to co-operate fully with the French and instead of joining the by now futile attack that the French had planned, he ordered his army to turn north and withdraw at once in the direction of Dunkirk. This decision, together with the question of whether or not Gort actually told the French of his plans in advance, has caused rancour and bitterness in France ever since.

Nevertheless, Gort had grasped the fact that if he allowed the BEF to be destroyed, there would be nothing else with which to defend Britain. The extraction of the British Army, as far as possible intact, now became his priority. His actions further reinforced the French view of 'perfidious Albion', and the belief that the British would fight, but only to the last Frenchman. Whatever the validity or otherwise of the French opinion, this one act by Gort undoubtedly helped save Great Britain from invasion.

Victor Clough was a member of the battalion transport section, but had thus far made his way towards Dunkirk on foot. He continues his account:

> Coming back, about ten miles outside of Armentières, the Military Police were commandeering lorries and putting us on them, and sending us down towards Dunkirk. I wouldn't say it was panic, but there wasn't much fighting – we were dodging the enemy. You walked at night and hid during the day. The only thing you could shoot at was German aircraft . . . we were bombed just out the other side of Armentières, they saw the

lorry, and of course everybody scattered, and they bombed some of the lorries . . . coming back we came across a troop of twenty-five-pounders, and the guns had got stuck in the mud, and they were going to blow the guns up.[29]

Gordon Spring's party continued their retreat and it was apparent to him that discipline in the BEF was breaking down:

We headed back a different way. The most dreadful order was given: 'Every man for himself!' The great British Army, bastion of state and Empire – all that we had learnt about at school. Here it was giving up the ghost. We had no time to ponder on the magnitude of what had been ordered. We met an officer who told us to head west for Dunkirk.

We were dive bombed. There was a God Almighty rush for any cover possible, usually a ditch. The place was littered with the bloody remains of horses and people. It was all stomach churning and gut wrenching stuff but you have to move on. A Colonel came up and said, 'You with the Bren Gun – shoot any man who discards his uniform.' I refused. I refused an order from a Colonel. This was anarchy. He threatened to court martial me but I told him I doubted whether we'd get back. Hope had begun to wane, you see. It must have done if I spoke so brazenly to a Colonel.

I saw a barn and said to all the men: 'Run for it.' The Colonel threatened to shoot us all – some hopes. I got to the barn and pulled a bale of straw over me. We rested for two days like that. Now the depression about your situation sets in. The world has turned upside down. All that you have held true and abided to in previous years has gone out of the window. Hunger is gnawing away at you.

We moved on and we came across a canteen. I helped myself to a tin of pears and condensed milk. Bad move – I was sick. We came to a gathering place where all the units under the sun seem to have washed up. I was ordered to go out with a sergeant from Yorkshire to scavenge like rats for food.

We got to this barn and dead tired fell asleep in the hayloft. When I woke up there were Germans below us. Bloody hell only yards from the enemy – instant death if they found us. We had to wait for dark, jump and leg it. We went over this field and a German Messerschmidt starts to machine gun us. We were saved by a shit pit that we both fell in. We came across another building. I did have a Thompson machine gun with me.

We approached it warily. Nothing there. We'd just turned around to leave and shots rang out. My sergeant was dead. Here one moment, gone the next. In anger I rushed back blasting away with my gun. I shot three of the bastards but then needed to get away myself. No shots followed me.

How I ever got back to the same bunch I'd been with I never knew – but I did – homing instinct perhaps. Yes that was it, you were now living on your nerves, your guile and wit. Almost all semblance of order had disappeared. All sorts of things flash through your mind but you haven't got time for this.[30]

Regimental Sergeant Major Edwin Ross had been with Richard Everard's party, but became separated from them when he went to try to help the Military Police clear refugees who were blocking a road. When he returned he found that the party he was with had gone.

Ross found himself more or less alone apart from a sergeant of the Military Police, who was keen to make headway as fast as possible towards Dunkirk. Ross, however, was having none of this, believing that if a soldier should become separated from his unit in the face of the enemy he should join the nearest operational unit. Ross as a Warrant Officer First Class held sway, and despite the protests of the sergeant the two men headed away from Dunkirk, towards the enemy.

In due course they attached themselves to a Scottish battalion, near Neuve Eglise, which was brewing tea whilst awaiting orders to advance. Whilst they were doing so, they came under German mortar fire and Ross was wounded by a splinter which struck him in the leg. The survivors of the Scots went forward into the attack, and were mostly captured, whilst stretcher bearers attended to Ross. Their temporary unit now out of action, Ross told the very relieved sergeant to make his way to Dunkirk alone, after giving him his money, spare socks and other supplies.

Private 'Moe' Harper, meanwhile, was still with part of B Company, which was withdrawing under the command of Major Ken Symington:

We withdrew again towards Lens & Armentières, refugees all clogging roads on our withdrawal line. A hopeless situation to be in. In Armentières two of us were given a Boys Anti-tank rifle, and told to set up in the railway yards to await the arrival of Boche tanks. That seemed OK, but we had no ammunition to fire. We did not receive any but were told to move again towards Dunkirk.[31]

Kenneth Ruddle continues his account of 27 May:

Having just got through POPERINGHE I got the troops under cover and sent back to STEENVORDE to try to find the brigade; this was without avail. I then sent a DR with an officer (2/Lt Ellis) on the back into DUNKIRK to see if movement control there could help me. We were bombed several times whilst waiting here ... Just after sending 2/Lt Ellis to DUNKIRK I met a major from 1st Division who told me that the BEF was being evacuated and that we should proceed to our divisional meeting point. I told him that I could not find my brigade or division and therefore could not find out where the meeting point was, so he suggested we should go to theirs (1st Division's). He assured me that the Military Police were patrolling all roads and that all troops would be pushed on to the coast so that I need not fear that the rest of the battalion would get left behind.

   We then pushed on towards 1st Division's meeting point and after meeting D.A.Q.M.G. 1st Division we were eventually pushed on towards LA PANNE having dumped our transport some miles back. We marched throughout the night.[32]

For those who had escaped the debacle on the canal, the stage was set now for the final act of the 1940 campaign in France. The most dramatic and audacious rescue of an army in British military history was about to take place, but for the men involved, much danger and drama still lay ahead.

Chapter 4

Dunkirk – the Cauldron of Hell

Sunday, 26 May 1940, the day upon which the Leicesters had fought their one-sided action on the canal, was a critical date in the story of the Battle of France. It was this date upon which the British War Cabinet, and Winston Churchill in particular, conceded that the military situation in northern France had now become critical. Field Marshal Gort had ordered his army to begin the withdrawal to the coast, and the Royal Navy, in the person of Admiral Bertram Ramsey, was instructed to commence Operation Dynamo, the code name for the evacuation of the BEF from France. The name, as every schoolboy knows, reflected the fact that Ramsey planned and commanded the operation from his headquarters in the Dynamo Room, situated on the white cliffs above Dover.

The Admiralty signal that commenced the operation marked the start of one of the greatest sea-borne endeavours in British history. Admiral Ramsey called in all the resources the Royal Navy could spare, along with all the civilian craft that could be mustered. Much has been made of the 'armada of little ships' that saved the BEF – the Sunday pleasure craft, the fishing boats etc. – but in truth, these small vessels simply did not have the 'muscle' to lift off troops in bulk. As always in war, the Royal Navy relied on the support of the Merchant Navy, in particular the thirty-six passenger ferries that were chartered by the Admiralty for this purpose. 'Chartered' is an important word because these vessels were not taken over by the Admiralty, but effectively hired for the job along with their crews, all of them civilians. They were about to sail into the very mouth of hell. Ramsey was initially sceptical about how many men the Navy could rescue, but the early forecasts were proved wrong and the numbers of British and French troops picked up eventually exceeded all expectations. This was in no small part due to the bravery of the Royal Navy and Merchant Navy crews.

The historic town of Dunkirk had been a popular holiday resort before the war, and its sandy beaches stretched some 20 miles eastwards from the town itself towards the mouth of the Yser River. Behind the beaches, the extensive sand dunes provided good assembly areas for troops to muster whilst they awaited evacuation. However, those same beaches were problematic because their shallow slope meant that not even smaller craft would be able to get in closer than about 100yd of the shore. This in turn meant that troops would either have to be rowed out to the rescue ships, or wade out to meet them in water that reached their chests. None of the three resorts along this stretch of coast (Malo-les-Bains, Bray Dunes and La Panne) had anything resembling a jetty or a pier. The evacuation of wounded from casualty clearing stations along the coast and of support personnel had actually begun several days earlier and Dunkirk had already received the attention of German bombers. In the port itself, the inner docks had already been destroyed by German bombing. There was an outer harbour, protected by two moles or breakwaters. Access to the West Mole was blocked by the town's oil terminal, which had also been bombed and was blazing fiercely. The East Mole, meanwhile, was connected to the beaches by a narrow causeway, but like its western neighbour it had been built purely as a breakwater. It was not designed to allow ships to dock alongside it.

During the final week of May 1940, this bombed and burning citadel became the focus of the human detritus of the German blitzkrieg, which had smashed a hole through the once proud British and French armies; armies that were now united only in defeat. Weary and despondent troops flooded in from the battlefields of northern France and Belgium. The appalling sight that met their eyes at Dunkirk was akin to a scene from Dante's *Inferno*. They were greeted by a panorama of burning oil tanks, smashed houses and shops, debris everywhere and thick black smoke billowing into the sky which stung the eyes and burnt the throat. It was not just the sight of wrecked and sinking vessels at the docks, or the sea in the harbour shimmering with a surface of diesel oil, that assaulted the senses. Equally shocking were the scenes of wretched humanity presented by the survivors of two once-mighty armies in which, in the humiliation of defeat, discipline had completely vanished. Drink was freely available from a dozen or more smashed cafes, and there had been much looting. The chief memory for many who passed through the wreckage of the town on their way back to Blighty that May and June of 1940 was of the copious quantities of free cigarettes. Thousands upon thousands of cartons were available from bombed warehouses, and the bedraggled survivors filled their pockets. Drunken soldiers occupied cellars and doorways, a mass of British, French and Senegalese, some of them lying in the road in their stupor, surrounded by vomit. British soldiers were seen staggering through the streets wearing women's hats and other apparel looted from abandoned shops.

The first of the flotilla of chartered Merchant Navy vessels to complete the round trip into this vision of hell as part of Operation Dynamo was SS *Mona's Isle*, an Isle of Man Steam Packet Company ferry. She was warned to sail on the morning of 26 May, but did not leave her position off the Downs until about 2100 hours that night. Her crew was told only that their mission was a dangerous one, and that once they reached their destination, the naval officer in charge would instruct them as to what they were to do. *Mona's Isle* reached Dunkirk at about 0400 hours on the morning of 27 May, and waited outside the harbour. Apart from the fires blazing in the town, there was little sign of activity and the crew wondered what they should do. Eventually they decided to berth within the harbour and await instructions. As it began to get light on that morning of 27 May, the first British troops appeared in the harbour and began to board. Private Dick Cobley was one of the first of the 2nd/5th Leicesters to embark, having hitched a ride with some members of the Royal Army Service Corps in a lorry that took him directly to Dunkirk. He too managed to get home with his quota of 'duty free' cigarettes:

> Travelling by lorry, mostly at night, we eventually reached the outskirts of Dunkirk. I had never heard of the place previously. I know we passed through Poperinghe and Armentières – all heavily bombed. Large oil tanks at Dunkirk were ablaze, planes were bombing and there were fires all around. The lorries were put out of action and we went into the town, picking our way through the rubble with telephone lines dangling every-where. We managed to get into a cellar where we stayed throughout the day. At night we were told to get down to the 'Mole' where we might get a ship. I remember passing a NAAFI store where we were told to help our-selves to cigarettes – everyone smoked in those days and I brought 400 Gold Flake back with me! We managed to get on a ship called the *Mona's Isle* – an Isle of Man ferry. We crowded on and it was standing room only and no life-jackets! I remember a sailor giving me some fried tomatoes which tasted lovely and we set sail from Dunkirk just before dawn.
>
> The ship went along the coast towards Calais which, unbeknown to the Captain, was already in German hands. Suddenly shells from the shore began to hit the ship and quite a lot found their target. Luckily we were down below – don't know if we could have got out. Then the planes came. They strafed the ship with cannon shells. Twenty-two men were killed and dozens wounded. There was nowhere to dodge to as it was so crowded, and when we eventually reached Dover it had taken over ten

hours to cross as the shells had damaged the steering. We saw that the ship's funnels were riddled with cannon shell holes – a good job they didn't have bombs! . . .

We, the lucky ones were put on a train to a tented camp at Tweseldown, near Ascot, where we were sorted out. It was hard to believe we were home, where only a few miles away our friends were still striving to get off the beaches.[1]

A plan had been agreed between the British and French generals commanding the Dunkirk garrisons to set up a defendable perimeter outside of the town, enclosing an area some 30 miles long by about 7 miles deep at the widest point, in order to hold off the Germans for as long as possible. The perimeter ran chiefly along the network of canals outside the town, but in some cases merely followed drainage ditches along the edges of fields where there was no more substantial obstacle available. The British held the eastern sector from Bergues to Nieuport-Bains, the French the western sector from Gravelines to Bergues. In many places the British sector was flooded, with the defenders having to make use of houses and other structures above ground. However, the flooding made the ground unsuitable for heavy armour which hampered the Germans – the network of canals also making movement difficult for the enemy tanks. Tiredness on the part of the German armies menacing the eastern sector (they had crossed Belgium without rest in a matter of days) may account for the lethargy and indecisiveness of the Germans at this point, factors that also worked to the advantage of the defenders. Nonetheless, had they really wished to, the Germans could probably have crushed the Dunkirk perimeter; what really saved the BEF was Hitler's famous (and controversial) 'Halt Order'. The Fuhrer was fearful that his panzers were outrunning their supplies, and he could scarcely believe that the British and French armies were as weak as they appeared to be. He worried that the Allies must be planning some sort of counterstroke and so halted the advance of the panzer armies for two vital days. He was later to claim in a radio broadcast in January 1945 that he had deliberately allowed the BEF to escape, as a sporting gesture, but like many of Hitler's claims, this had little basis in either truth or reality.

Throughout the following days a seemingly endless column of troops, some battered and bloodied from their encounters with the Germans, but all of them weary, reached this perimeter. Some travelled on foot but others arrived in a bizarre convoy of vehicles, from commandeered dustcarts, civilian cars and tractors to an endless number of British Army trucks. One of these latter vehicles was driven by a soldier from A Company of the 2nd/5th Leicesters, Lance Corporal Syd Garner, who arrived at Dunkirk with the outside of his 1,500-weight truck so festooned with troops that he could hardly see where he was going through the windscreen for the dangling legs. Arrival within the Dunkirk perimeter, however, meant that the exhausted survivors exchanged one set of problems for another. Away from the roads choked with refugees, they were at least free from the imminent threat of capture, but the pitiless air strikes on the blazing town meant that death was still close at hand even if other perils had temporarily been averted.

On 27 and 28 May, the bulk of the evacuation effort was focused on the beaches. However, the process of embarking men into whalers at the water's edge, rowing them out to ships that they then boarded via scramble nets, while the whalers returned to the shore for more men, was painfully slow. It might take a whaler 10 trips to embark 250 men, and whilst this was going on, the larger ship waiting at anchor further out was at tremendous risk of attack from the Luftwaffe. Private Harold Simons of A Company was evacuated in this way:

> We were in groups with other soldiers, really disorderly ... There were all sorts trying to scramble back. It was a disorderly thing, and when you got back to the water it was more disorderly! Nine times out of ten you got rid of your rifle, as you're not going to carry that in the water are you? Dunkirk was in chaos, being bombed and shelled, of course the Jerries had got the upper hand. You heard rumours come through, 'you're being evacuated, you're being evacuated', you know. We made our way to the beach, we were there twenty-four hours or more, but time doesn't mean anything there, and you were getting bombed and shelled ... You couldn't organise it. There might have been some sergeant or sergeant major shouting form a line, but you took no notice of him, it were every man for his self. I went into the water about chest high for a start, then a small boat came and picked us up. A rowing boat I think – there were lots of little boats came from across the water, little paddle boats and all sorts – a little family boat came in and took about half a dozen of us out to a bigger ship, a Royal Navy ship. We got no dry clothes, not till we got to Blighty ... We were machine gunned by Messerschmidts and they put some shells over ...[2]

Lieutenant Colonel Kenneth Ruddle's account continues from his arrival at La Panne at about 0400 hours on 28 May:

I reported to a Brigadier who was controlling the embarkation and we were ordered to remain in some nearby orchards. At about 1430 hours we were called upon to proceed with other troops (which were put under my command) about two to three miles and line a canal as the enemy were reported to be advancing from FURNES. We were machine gunned from the air just before moving off. We then moved off in a terrific thunderstorm and everyone was soaked to the skin. On arrival at the canal I decided on the disposition of the troops and left two other officers to get their Coys into position whilst I returned to the Brigadier to try to get more ammunition and to enquire re any orders re withdrawing etc. As I was doing this I met my QM who brought a message ordering our withdrawal as the enemy had been repulsed some miles away. Its very doubtful whether the whole scare was not the work of the 5th column. We then returned to LA PANNE and did the best we could to dry ourselves. We were ordered on to 'C' Beach at 2145 hrs that evening and shortly afterwards began to wade out to boats in small parties.[3]

Meanwhile, the main body of the 2nd/5th Leicesters, comprising some seventy men and four officers under the command of Major Ken Symington, remained under the direct authority of 139th Brigade. The brigade continued to attempt to fight as an organised formation and this party was the only portion of the 2nd/5th still trying to withdraw in an orderly fashion towards the coast. The 139th Brigade war diary reveals that on 27 May the rump of the 2nd/5th battalion were at Winnezeele, close to the Franco-Belgian border, but the following day, 28 May, they were ordered to withdraw within the Dunkirk perimeter and to act as a rearguard to remainder of the 46th Division. At 1300 hours on 28 May they began to withdraw and proceeded via Bambecque and Vyfweg, where their transport was abandoned, and crossed the Bergues–Furnes Canal into the Dunkirk perimeter.

Late on 28 May, Admiral Ramsey switched the emphasis of the evacuation to the East Mole. This was to prove a far quicker method of embarking troops. If a destroyer could come alongside the Mole – not an easy task in itself even for an experienced destroyer captain – around 900 men could be embarked in a relatively short space of time. Private Jim Hall of Burbage had by this time reached Dunkirk, courtesy of the Royal Engineers sappers with whom he had scrounged a lift on a truck. He takes up the story:

On the outskirts of Dunkirk we were stopped by some Military Police, who told the driver to dump the truck in a field. There were hundreds of them, or so it seemed. They then sent the Engineers on their way into Dunkirk, and me being in the bloody infantry had to stay! When they had a good sized crowd of infantry (all types and different regiments) we had to go with an officer to a canal or dyke where we were part of the rearguard action. The only problem was there wasn't much action.

We were there about a day and then told to get into the town and down to the docks. I went through the town and it was in ruins. It was still being bombed and shelled. One night time we were told to get on to the Mole, which was a long jetty going out into the sea. It was badly damaged by shells or bombs. As I was going along it I heard someone shout 'here mate'. Looking down I saw a small boat. I got down and in the boat was an RN rating and a civvy. I think there were about eight or nine in the boat when they took us out to sea, and put us on a larger boat. I was the first on, and told to go down to the hold which was empty.

I sat down and I was out like a light! When I woke up the hold was full of soldiers both British and French. I got up on deck which was full of Frenchmen, and it was by now daylight. Some Hurricanes flew by us towards France and I remember one of them dipping its wings in salute and there in front of us was Blighty![4]

Lieutenant Richard Everard and Captain Geoff Gee, having put their men on some passing transport, had hitched a ride themselves in an empty 3-tonner. Dawn on 29 May found them shivering in the back after getting wet through in a thunder storm the previous evening. Everard takes up the story:

There was another endless traffic jam. We decided to walk and get warm. We had an idea we were about seven or eight miles from Dunkirk which we could see burning in the distance. We tramped through the confusion – trucks, French, British marching troops and all the debris of war. In the fields by the side of the road trucks and equipment of all kinds were being destroyed so that it should not fall into enemy hands. The road was being heavily shelled by now so we cut across country. We came at last to the outskirts of Dunkirk. We met a man in a priest's cassock who held out his arms to stop us and said in French that Dunkirk was being guarded by French bayonets. We were too browned off to take any notice of him. We got another lift in a truck. A plane tried hard to bomb us. We thought it was quite near enough so we decided to keep on our feet. We got into the centre of Dunkirk; the chaos was indescribable. No one knew what was happening and the town was being heavily shelled and bombed. Someone

> said they thought we were being evacuated so we made for the beach.
> There were thousands of men in long queues. We met some people with
> food and about 9.00am we had a breakfast of chocolate and tinned
> asparagus![5]

Everard was quick to see the comic side of this, and there were other men at
Dunkirk who later recounted the sheer irony of opening unmarked tins in
desperation and finding that they contained the finest caviar, which in peacetime they would never have encountered. Hunger, however, was a real problem
now for the troops awaiting evacuation. Supply lines had completely broken
down, and the 2nd/5th battalion as far back as 25 May had been informed that
it was now to live off the land as best it could. Some men had been without
proper food for almost a week. Lance Corporal Syd Garner, the transport
driver from A Company, and his mates came upon a 14-pound chunk of corned
beef lying among the dunes. In spite of the fact it was soaked in diesel oil they
carved it up with their bayonets and ate it voraciously, such was their hunger.[6]
Garner went on to serve in North Africa and the Italian campaign, and fought
at Monte Cassino, but he told his family in later years that for him Dunkirk was
the worst experience of the entire war.

Lieutenant Richard Everard, still on 29 May, was now on the beach awaiting
his turn to embark:

> The naval officer who was in charge of the beaches was very calm, very
> orderly and certainly getting the job done ... There was a lot of bombing
> but, considering the thousands of men jammed together, there was not a
> high proportion of casualties. Everyone behaved very well. Then, to our
> joy, six Spitfires came over; they were the first British planes we had seen
> in the past fourteen days. There was more bombing, more wounded.
> In long seemingly endless lines we moved slowly on. We reached the
> mole; more bombing. We got on a ship. It was the cross channel steamer
> *Canterbury*. There was a destroyer alongside. We got on board about
> 2.00pm. There was more bombing – some very near misses. Some
> German airmen were brought on board. They were nearly lynched but
> they behaved very well and were sent to bring in men who had just been
> wounded. The AA (Anti-Aircraft) gunners in the ship brought down a
> Jerry plane. That bucked everyone up and all on board blazed off with
> anything they had got whatever the height of the plane. If it did nothing
> else it relieved one's feelings. Mike Moore was brought on board on a
> stretcher. At 4.00pm we upped anchor and away. Shore batteries North of

town, and only recently captured from the French, opened on us. The destroyer replied. We zig zagged about and got under way full steam ahead. We took a course due North. There was nothing we could do on deck, so we went below to the lounge and had afternoon tea and thin bread and butter. We had a long way to go, and finally arrived at Dover at midnight. We sent telegrams to our wives who, incidentally, thought we were still in Brittany.

After a bit of waiting we got into a train and later arrived at Aldershot. We had breakfast, a good wash and changed into borrowed clothes. We were granted forty-eight hours leave provided we did not use any public transport, so Geoff and I hired a car and later in the afternoon we were in our own homes.[7]

In fact, Captain Geoff Gee's own memories add further detail to the story of his and Everard's evacuation. His family recall a story of the *Canterbury* actually being hit by a bomb, which went down the ship's funnel but failed to go off. If it had, the consequences would have been disastrous, as they were for the SS *Lancastria* at St Nazaire. A bomb down her funnel blew the bottom out of the vessel. Packed with troops, she sank rapidly with great loss of life.

Mike Moore had been lucky to be taken on board. As the evacuation progressed, a decision was taken to leave stretcher cases behind and give preference to the able-bodied. In field hospitals and dressing stations, lots were drawn by medics to decide who would remain with the wounded to care for them until the Germans arrived. Regimental Sergeant Major Ross, who arrived in Dunkirk by ambulance, was another stretcher case who was fortunate to be embarked when so many others were not.

Meanwhile, on the outskirts of the town, dawn on 29 May found the main body of the 2nd/5th Leicesters holding the Bergues Canal line at Coudekerque. Once again they were tasked with defending a crossing point. One of the men holding the line here was a 21-year-old soldier from Birstall, Private Harry Crane. He remembered later that the men were cold, hungry and exhausted. The party mustered only fourteen rifles between them and ten rounds of ammunition per man. A message came through asking the men to 'stick it out' for as long as possible, but left the men under no illusion that they would be sacrificed if necessary to allow better trained and equipped formations time to evacuate.

One of the officers here was battalion signals officer Lieutenant Jack Townsend, also only 21. His party of signallers, many of whom had never fired a rifle, were hastily retrained as infantrymen and shown the rudiments of the .303 Short Magazine Lee-Enfield rifle. He remembered moving up and down the line, chatting to the men and attempting to keep their spirits up as their eyes and ears strained for the sight of enemy infantry or rumble of tanks on the pavé road. The officers were attempting to put a brave face on things, though Townsend admitted years later that all of them, himself included, were frightened. He read the message out to the men, and received some well-chosen comments from them about what exactly GHQ could do with it! They were destined to hold this position for some thirty-six hours in all.

Lieutenant Colonel Kenneth Ruddle, meanwhile, had been shepherding his composite force onto boats on C Beach. His account continues:

> We were still wading out in the early hours of 29th and eventually I left with the last party at about 0400 hours. I was transferred to a motor boat, which broke down, and then to another motor boat and then to a mine-sweeper. There, the navy gave me a change of clothes and hot drinks etc. I soon had to transfer again however to a destroyer (the *Calcutta* – which had brought back the 1/5th Leicestershire Regt from Norway) and as most of my clothes had been lost in the process of drying, had to do so in grey flannels and a naval blue sweater and battledress blouse.
>
> The destroyer remained off LA PANNE for several hours, taking more on board and eventually we sailed and in spite of several air raid warnings arrived at SHEERNESS without incident that evening.
>
> I had expected to find all my party on the same destroyer but they were all on different ones and there were only two or three of my men on the train that left SHEERNESS. We were taken to CHISLEDON CAMP, arriving there about 0400 hrs on May 30th.[8]

The 30th was a particularly good day for the evacuation – the day was misty with low cloud. Visibility was so poor that the Luftwaffe was effectively grounded all day. Troops packed the small causeway leading onto the Mole and a constant stream moved along it, averaging a thousand men an hour. Numbers lifted from the beaches also increased dramatically on 30 May, partly because the lack of enemy air activity meant that ships could wait off shore in relative safety and so were less likely to leave without waiting until they were fully loaded. In addition, early on 30 May the Royal Engineers had constructed a makeshift pier at Bray Dunes, by driving a line of trucks as far as they could out to sea and then decking them with planks. A similar feature was constructed at La Panne. This of course provided an alternative method of embarking troops from the beaches without the time-consuming process of rowing them out, and without the risk of using the Mole.

Private Gordon Spring and his companions, upon reaching the town, drove their trucks into a field and set fire to them. They then made their way into the town, hoping to be able to board a ship. In fact, several such groups of men who had become detached from their own units found that this was a distinct disadvantage when it came to boarding vessels. One group of fifty or more men made up of stragglers queued up patiently on the beach only to be told by the beach master at the head of the queue that he was not taking 'odds and sods', giving preference instead to complete units. This happened to some groups more than once and the effect was demoralising to say the least. This appears to have been what happened to Gordon Spring. He remembered:

> What a scene of chaos and madness. The acrid smoke in our nostrils, our burning hunger and sheer amazement that others had made it. For three nights I approached the East Wharf for the pier only to be turned back. We were subject to constant attacks from the air which made it a complete lottery as to whether you survived or not ... I pulled a chap from a burning truck and I had to pull bodies out of the sea. The Padre was killed near me and there was nothing for it but to administer something of the last rights to those poor devils. This was our army – shattered in mind and limb, without form or order.[9]

Other men of the 2nd/5th drifted into Dunkirk in dribs and drabs. Lance Corporal Ron Riches of Uppingham reached the town after a long journey across country. Men either side of him had been killed by German machine-gun fire, but he and a group of comrades eventually made it to the beach. Not wishing to wait in long lines up to shoulder deep in the sea as other small parties were forced to do – exposed to German air attack and at risk of being turned back – Riches and his comrades decided to swim out to a minesweeper, which took them to Ramsgate. Back safely on the Kent coast, the gunfire from Dunkirk was still clearly audible. Another isolated group came in with Sergeant John Dwyer, a Liverpudlian who had seen previous service with the Manchester Regiment in India in the 1930s. With no work to be had on Merseyside, Dwyer had moved to Leicester in search of employment. A talented musician, he had joined the band of the 2nd/5th Leicesters before the outbreak of war, and like many Army bandsmen served with his battalion in France in 1940 as a stretcher bearer. Dwyer and his party were eventually evacuated aboard HMS *Greyhound*, but the campaign had taken its toll on him. The chaos of the preceding weeks had meant that a perforated stomach ulcer had remained untreated, and this ultimately led to Dwyer's discharge from the Army.

Lance Corporal Ronald Webster of Coalville (known in the battalion as 'Clem') and his party reached the beaches with only one rifle between four men. Rather than wait in lines with the rest of the infantry on the beach, Webster decided to take his chances. Abandoning his uniform on the beach, he swam for over a mile to a waiting rescue vessel, and climbed aboard with just his boots tied around his neck. On the way, he was machine-gunned in the water by a low flying Messerschmidt skimming the waves, though he was unhurt. Finally arriving back in England, he received the princely sum of 3*s* 6*d* in back pay for each of the weeks that he had been in France! Another soldier evacuated was Private Arthur Knight, of Donnington Street, Leicester. Arthur was a bright lad, idolised by his younger sister. Although he had passed the eleven-plus exam, his family could not afford for him to stay on at school. From the age of 16 he had worked at the Corah knitwear company in Leicester, but just prior to the war had passed an exam to join a railway company. His call-up papers arrived before he could take up the job, and he left for war. Although he survived the ordeal on the beaches of Dunkirk, he went on to serve in the Italian campaign, and lost his life near Monte Cassino.

Sergeant Ian Noble had managed to bring his small party within the Dunkirk perimeter, having lost only one man during the retreat. They waited for several days on the beach, passing the time by digging scrapes in the sand, lying on their backs and taking pot shots at enemy aircraft with their .303 Lee-Enfield rifles until their ammunition ran out. They were, he recalled many years later, unconcerned by the Stuka dive bombers, as unless they scored a direct hit, the destructive force of their bombs was dissipated by the soft sand. Messerschmidt Me109s, however, were a different story, and their strafing runs along the beach firing machine guns caused the majority of the casualties among the waiting troops. Whilst the Royal Navy's efforts in bombarding German forces on the shore gave them heart, the apparent lack of RAF fighter cover over the beaches disgusted them.

On 30 May, Noble was evacuated via the Mole on to a destroyer. He was not, however, out of danger yet, as the vessel was attacked by enemy aircraft as it left the port. Although the ship was not hit, Noble suffered the indignity of having his battledress trousers blown off by a near miss. A sympathetic sailor gave him a spare set of Royal Navy bell-bottom trousers and he arrived back in

England thus attired. News quickly reached him that his pregnant wife had in fact given birth to their first son three days earlier, whilst Noble was on the Dunkirk beaches. Dishevelled and filthy, still covered in sand and not having washed or shaved for many days, he nonetheless rushed straight to the hospital. His wife, meanwhile, was blissfully unaware of his ordeal. In the hospital news of the unfolding debacle in France had been kept from her, and she was not aware that at one point her husband had actually been posted as 'missing, believed killed'. Upon reaching the maternity ward, his wife's first words to him were, 'Christ, Ian, you stink!'[10]

In addition to the ever-present attentions of the Luftwaffe, the only respite from whose fighters and bombers came when poor weather temporarily halted their strafing runs, the troops waiting in the dunes and on the beaches were subjected to propaganda intended to demoralise them even further. Pieces of paper blowing about amid the dunes and by the sides of the road were picked up by many British troops, and turned out to be German propaganda leaflets. They were printed with a map showing the Channel coast on one side, and on the other the chilling text: 'British Soldiers! Look at this map, it gives your true situation! Your troops are entirely surrounded! Stop Fighting! Put down your arms!'[11] Other German leaflets needled the Tommies over their apparent lack of RAF air cover, or taunted them that their generals had already gone home and left them.

On 1 June during the afternoon, the last remaining part of the 2nd/5th Leicesters still fighting as a formation, the garrison at Coudekerque, was ordered by 139th Brigade to withdraw to the beaches and begin to embark. Lieutenant Jack Townsend remembered the sense of relief he experienced when the dispatch rider appeared and the orders for which they had been waiting finally arrived. After throwing their virtually useless rifles into the canal, they began marching the final mile into the town. Dunkirk itself was blazing fiercely now and the bodies of those men who had been killed in earlier bombardments had been laid at the sides of the road. Even for men like Townsend, for whom the previous week had been a rapid introduction to the reality of warfare, it was a shocking sight. Townsend and his men waited 5 hours on the Mole before, under cover of darkness, the destroyer HMS *Windsor* arrived. The waiting men were almost too many for her to cope with, and she was dangerously overloaded as she withdrew towards England. Private Harry Crane, meanwhile, was picked up just after midnight by the destroyer HMS *Codlington*.

The operation to evacuate the BEF was reaching its climax now, with the total of 64,000 men lifted on 1 June only marginally less than what was achieved on 31 May under ideal conditions. By 2 June the numbers tailed off dramatically to 26,000. Private 'Moe' Harper remembered:

> On June 2nd we were told to make our own way to Dunkirk for our evacuation. Chaos at Dunkirk, fires everywhere, we were eventually sent to the beach at La Panne. Tried several times to board a boat being bombed and machine gunned by Stukas all day. No luck, so decided to stay the night in the sand dunes, to try our luck next day.
>
> There were only four of us from our unit together now. My small group eventually made it to the front of our queue, loaded into a boat and [were] taken a short trip and transferred to a paddle steamer which had got quite close in, the *Royal Eagle*, which sailed the Thames to Southend and Margate during peacetime. The boat was packed, I managed to find a small space alongside the funnel. I stripped off (as I was soaked) and started to dry out, looking forward to moving off . . . Alas the tide went out, and we were left high and dry on the beach. A message [broadcast] over the Tannoy asking for volunteers to scan the beaches for ammunition for the boat's Lewis machine guns and men to fill the belts for the same was soon answered.
>
> I did three trips, two with ammunition, and a third trip . . . walking along the beach I found a khaki painted tin (contents unknown) about 2 feet deep by 1 foot square. I staggered back to the boat with this and carried it back on board (still beached) and asked a crew member what to do with it. He said, take it to the galley, I did as told and the contents turned out to be sugar, hence its weight. The galley cooks gave me two loaves of bread and two tins of Bully Beef for my find, so the four Tigers sat on the wide stairs of the boat, enjoying our first meal for days.
>
> By this time the tide had turned and was well on the way in again. After waiting about another hour, orders [came] over the tannoy. Organised rocking of the boat, under instructions, port side then starboard to try to free the keel. After about half a dozen rocks we were free, a big cheer went up, and we were on our way to Blighty. During our stay on the beach, our Lewis gunners shot down three Stukas. This was reported in the *Daily Mirror* as 'The *Royal Eagle*, scuttler of dive bombers'.
>
> We eventually arrived at Harwich, caught the train and finished up in our own regimental barracks at Glen Parva.[12]

Great forbearance and patience was shown by men who had been through so much already as they lay waiting those last few hours amid the bombing and flames. Private Alf Nichols of South Wigston remembered:

> We went on to the pier to board a ship, when there was an air attack. We had to retreat back on to the sands. We took shelter [in a dug out] in which we had a dead horse lying above us. In the shelter I found a prayer book, which I read, and prayed ... twenty-four hours later a rescue ship, the SS *St Helier*, came in and we eventually sailed ... there was only myself and Private Bradley from the Leicesters to the best of my knowledge on the ship. The main body of the Leicesters had caught earlier boats ... as for food and drink, as far as I can recall we had nothing from the time we left the canal, to setting foot in England ... one incident I do recall – we asked if we could help out as stretcher-bearers [while we waited], but was told we could if we gave up our rifles and that I was not prepared to do. I had my rifle with me, all the way through, only for it to get stolen the first night back in Aldershot barracks.[13]

Private Harry Hollier, of Earl Howe Street, Leicester, and a member of the *Leicester Evening Mail* stereotype department before the war, spent his twenty-first birthday awaiting evacuation. He endured intense bombing as he waited his turn to be picked up, yet by the time one of the final rescue vessels arrived and he embarked, this had all but died away and he spent an uneventful voyage asleep. Yet for some men, the strain of the whole experience, of days of battle, retreat, the lack of food and sleep, had become too much to bear. Private Gordon Spring remembered:

> I found a canoe to paddle with my helmet but it sank. I tried to get out to a battleship and did so only to find it struck by a shell and going nowhere. I had to go back to the beach – exhausted after my efforts. In all this hell, our humanity remained somewhere deep inside. We sang 'Onward Christian Soldiers' around a piano to momentarily lift the spirits. We were then dive bombed and I got shrapnel in each shoulder. The bloke next to me was trying to get up. All his bowels were hanging out. I cried – for the first time.
>
> I cracked. I am not ashamed of it – I cracked. I shouted out with all my strength and energy, 'Please God let me die now'. This is what I had come to. A bright lad, respectful of authority and a loving son and brother. My

moment of utter desperation and darkness. I had reached the depths of the inferno and the flames were searing at my skin and bones.[14]

At a few minutes to midnight on 2 June, the Channel Islands ferry *St Helier* left the Mole for the final time and made for England. She was the last vessel to take part in the 'official' evacuation. Shortly afterwards the naval officer conducting operations at Dunkirk boarded a cutter to tour the beaches. As he did so, he shouted through a megaphone to any remaining British stragglers who might have been left in the dunes. No one answered his calls – the only British soldiers left now it seemed were dead. The French still held on (a gallant rearguard holding the Germans outside Dunkirk at bay until the early hours of 4 June) and in fact with the evacuation of the BEF complete, a number of British ships did still return on 3 June with the express intention of taking off as many French soldiers as possible.

Gordon Spring was quite clearly suffering from shell shock – battle fatigue, or post-traumatic stress disorder as it might be termed today. The events of the previous week had been too much for him and this coupled with lack of food and proper rest had brought him to the point of collapse. He had no clear recollection of how he left Dunkirk, other than the fact that when the craft in which he travelled reached Dover on 3 June, he was carried off by the French troops who had also crossed with him, and who presumably had also put him in the boat on the French side. It seems likely that Spring was evacuated with the French troops after Operation Dynamo had officially ended.

Private Victor Clough was one of the last British soldiers to leave Dunkirk, and almost certainly the last member of the 2nd/5th to leave via this port. The story of his escape is among the most remarkable. His small party arrived there on 3 June to find the fields outside the town strewn with burning vehicles. The Military Police had pierced the sumps of the engines with a pick axe, run the engines till they seized, then poured petrol inside them and set them alight. Anti-aircraft guns had been spiked, stores unable to be carried had been destroyed. Nothing of potential value to the enemy was left behind. That evening the evacuation was effectively over, and Clough and his companions found no ships waiting for them. However, the small band decided that it was better to try to escape, and risk the treacherous currents of the Channel, than simply wait to be captured:

> In the town itself is a cement factory, with an iron bridge. That was the only bridge that wasn't blown up, it was a footbridge, and everybody was

German troops make an assault crossing of a canal using rubber dinghies, May 1940. It was craft such as these that the Germans used to cross the Deule Canal, and which they later used to ferry the prisoners back. (*Taylor Library*)

French Senegalese POWs being marched to the rear. It was the sudden withdrawal of Senegalese troops that allowed the Germans to outflank the Leicesters, and which precipitated the disaster of 26 May 1940. (*Author's collection*)

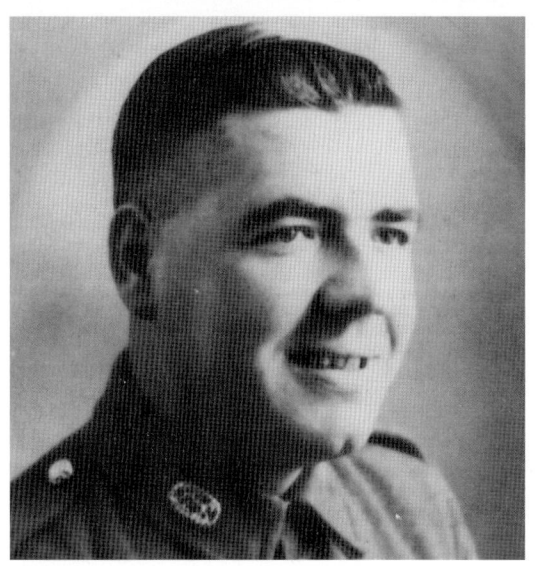

Corporal Andrew Quigley of Lutterworth, C Company Bren gunner. He was killed in action on 26 May 1940 and later received a posthumous Mention in Despatches. (*Mr A. Quigley*)

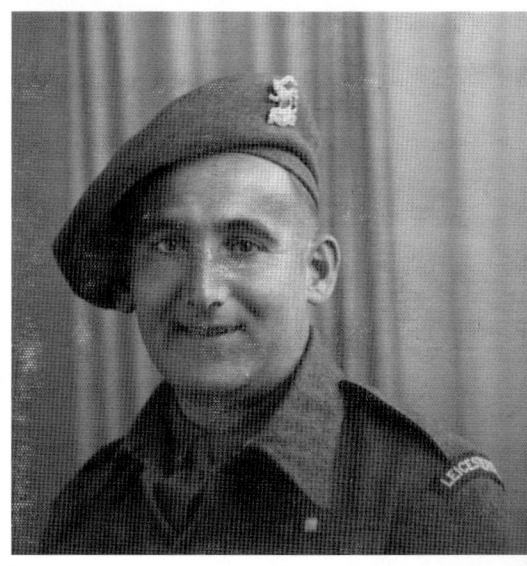

Private Don French, a hosiery hand, of Kibworth. He was wounded in the left shoulder and captured on 26 May 1940. (*Author's collection*)

The triage slip given to Don French in hospital after treatment for his wounded shoulder. (*Author's collection*)

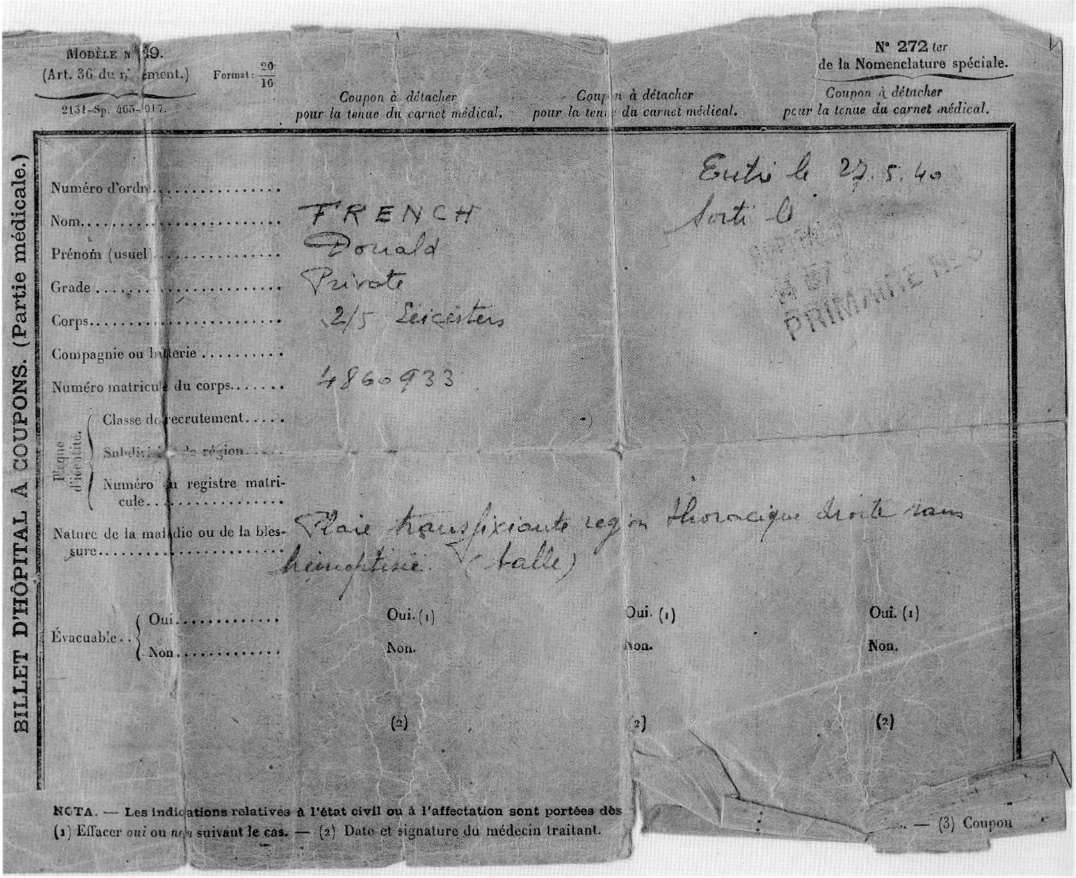

MODÈLE N° 19.
(Art. 36 du r[èglement.])
2131-Sp. 465-917.
Format : 20/16

Coupon à détacher pour la tenue du carnet médical.
Coupon à détacher pour la tenue du carnet médical.

N° 272 *ter* de la Nomenclature spéciale.
Coupon à détacher pour la tenue du carnet médical.

BILLET D'HÔPITAL A COUPONS. (Partie médicale.)

Entré le 27.5.40
Sorti le

Numéro d'ordre
Nom FRENCH
Prénom (usuel) Donald
Grade Private
Corps 2/5 Leicesters
Compagnie ou batterie
Numéro matricule du corps 4860933
Plaque d'identité: Classe de recrutement / Subdivision de région / Numéro du registre matricule
Nature de la maladie ou de la blessure: Plaie transfixiante région thoracique droite sans hémoptisie (balle)

Évacuable: Oui / Non
Oui. (1) Non. (2)
Oui. (1) Non. (2)
Oui. (1) Non. (2)

NOTA. — Les indications relatives à l'état civil ou à l'affectation sont portées dès
(1) Effacer *oui* ou *non* suivant le cas. — (2) Date et signature du médecin traitant.
— (3) Coupon

Private Joseph Gamble, D Company, of Barwell, killed in action on 26 May 1940. (*Author's collection*)

Private Phil Haywood. An engineer by trade, he had poor sight in one eye and joined the 2nd/5th Leicesters as a bandsman. He was captured on 26 May 1940. (*Mrs J. Haywood*)

Private Freddie Diaper of Leicester, killed in action on 26 May. His young widow Nellie had been married to him for only a few months. (*Mrs J. Richardson*)

Private Dick Cobley, who returned from Dunkirk with 400 Gold Flake cigarettes. (*Author's collection*)

Lieutenant Richard Everard. He and Captain Geoff Gee were the 'last men out of Lille' before the town's bridges were blown up ahead of the advancing Germans. (*Mr R. Everard*)

Private Harold Simons, who joined the 2nd/5th battalion in April 1940. He remembered the retreat to Dunkirk as 'a disorderly affair', which got more disorderly as it went on. (*Mr H. Simons*)

The canal at Coudekerque on the Dunkirk perimeter, looking north. The right bank here was held for two days in June 1940 by the seventy-strong main body of the 2nd/5th battalion, under Major Ken Symington and Lieutenant Jack Townsend. (*Author's collection*)

Private Harry Crane, of Leicester. He was part of the seventy-man garrison at Coudekerque. (*Mrs A. Martin*)

The Isle of Man Steam Packet vessel *Mona's Isle*, the first rescue ship into Dunkirk and the vessel that picked up Dick Cobley. (*Author's collection*)

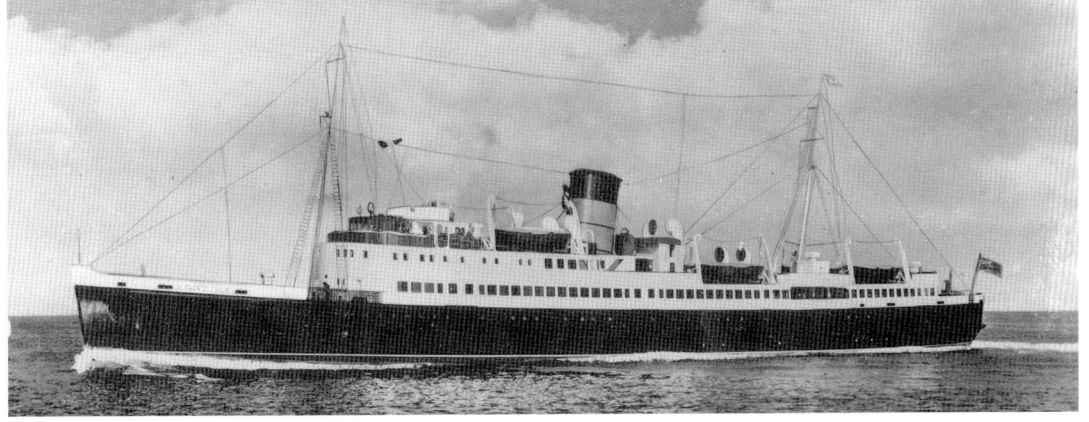

Sergeant Ian C. Noble. He lost his battledress trousers during the Dunkirk evacuation and returned home wearing sailor's bell-bottoms. (*Captain K. Noble*)

Private Alf Nichols, of South Wigston. He found a Bible on the beach at Dunkirk and prayed. (*Mr G. Nichols*)

SS *Royal Eagle*, aboard which 'Moe' Harper returned from Dunkirk. The vessel destroyed two Stukas whilst in the harbour. (*Author's collection*)

The Channel Islands ferry *St Helier*, which carried Alf Nichols from Dunkirk. (*Author's collection*)

Private Gordon Spring, of Hinckley. The stress of battle brought him to the brink of mental collapse at Dunkirk. (*Mr G. Spring*)

Lance Corporal Sid Garner, of A Company. On the beach at Dunkirk he was so hungry that he ate corned beef soaked in diesel oil. (*Mrs M. Garner*)

Private Arthur Knight, who survived the Dunkirk evacuation only to lose his life in Italy. (*Mrs I. Malin*)

Lance Corporal Ron Riches of Uppingham and his bride. (*Mrs B. Riches*)

Sergeant John Dwyer, bandsman and battalion stretcher bearer. He returned from Dunkirk with a perforated ulcer. (*Mr T. Dwyer*)

Lance Corporal Ronald 'Clem' Webster, of Coalville. He swam out to a British vessel, being machine-gunned by German aircraft as he did so. (*Mr M. Findley*)

Private Victor Clough, of Houghton on the Hill. One of the last to reach Dunkirk, he and his party found an abandoned rowing boat and took their chances with the Channel currents. (*Mr V. Clough*)

Regimental Quartermaster Sergeant Joe French DCM. He was probably the last Tiger to escape from France in June 1940. (*Mr J. French*)

going over that down to the beaches ... We were all totally mixed up, there were no regiments ... There was hardly anyone on the beach by then, [only] a load of wounded and various scattered groups. There was no organisation then ... There was nobody really in charge. We walked along the beach and there was two sailors with us, and we came across this boat that was floating, not a dingy, more a small boat. Well, we climbed on board, there was four oars on the boat. We discussed it, and decided we were not going to stay there ... It was getting dusk, so we got in the boat, there was eight of us, we started rowing, and of course we'd got no compass, nothing like that, so what we had to do was turn our back on the flames and all the ruins, and started rowing. Just after dawn a destroyer came along – we didn't know if it was a British one or a German one, until a bloke said, 'What are you doing here?' We said we were trying to get to England. He said 'Well you'd better hop on board!'.[15]

Clough's boat was probably one of those being used to row troops on the beach out to larger ships, abandoned after its last trip. The destroyer dropped his party off at Dover, and Clough made his way to a reception camp. By an amazing coincidence, of the 300,000 or more men evacuated from the Dunkirk beaches, Clough then bumped into his neighbour from across the road in Houghton on the Hill, who was serving in a Guards regiment. Both men wanted to send telegrams to their next of kin, but only Clough had any money. He remembered years later the friend's mother had run across the road to his house waving her telegram and shouting, 'Victor's safe and I've got to give you a shilling!'

Through every town and village through which the Dunkirk survivors passed bunting was strewn and flags were waved. Cups of tea and buns were thrust through carriage windows at every station at which the trains stopped. Chalked graffiti on the walls proclaimed 'Well Done BEF' and other such sentiments. The British press was in no doubt as to the national mood of relief and jubilation, which fell little short of triumphal at times. The *Daily Express* trumpeted, 'Tired, dirty, hungry, they came back – unbeatable.' The *Daily Mirror* was blunter still, its headline reading simply, 'Bloody Marvellous'! There was, however, a darker side to this national sense of jubilation. Now out of imminent danger, many of the men who had endured day upon day of air attack and shelling, not to mention what they may have experienced in the days of fighting prior to the evacuation, began to suffer the effects of prolonged emotional stress. The Army warned womenfolk darkly not to worry unduly if their menfolk did not seem themselves or if they reacted violently to sudden loud noises or aircraft flying low over their homes.

With the BEF out of France, Prime Minister Winston Churchill was still full of fight and entertaining schemes for landing British forces further along the French coast, but this was fantasy. The best units in the French Army had been destroyed in the north along with the strongest armour and most of France's heavy guns. Those French forces that remained active were the weakest. On 10 June the French government abandoned Paris and made for Bordeaux. Paris was declared an open city and German panzers rolled down the Champs Elysee. The rest was a foregone conclusion. On 22 June 1940, utterly demoralised, the French generals signed an Armistice at Compiègne, in the same railway carriage that had been used to sign the 1918 ceasefire documents. France was partitioned and three-fifths (that portion containing all of the French Atlantic ports and all of the industrial and coal-producing areas of the north) were occupied by Germany. For Hitler this was a triumph. The French monument commemorating victory here twenty-two years earlier was destroyed on his orders, and the carriage taken to Germany as a trophy.

Perhaps the last of all of the 2nd/5th Leicesters to leave France was Regimental Quartermaster Sergeant Joe French. He was in command of a small party that was still isolated in France after the French government had signed the Armistice with Germany. They commandeered a French locomotive, and ordered the driver to take them to Cherbourg where they hoped to re-embark for England. The terms of the Armistice required the French to hand over any foreign nationals on their soil to the Germans, and it was stated by many of those who were still in France at this point in time that the attitude of ordinary French men and women towards the British changed almost overnight, to one of open hostility. At one point in his journey, Joe French noticed that the train was heading in the wrong direction, and later when they stopped for water, being a good linguist he questioned the driver. He was not satisfied with the answers that the driver gave, and so contrived to listen in secretly to a conversation between the fireman and the driver. Aghast, he learned that they were both collaborationists, planning to take the British soldiers to the German lines and hand them over. He shot them both, and a locomotive driver was found from among the British soldiers on the train. They reached Cherbourg, where they commandeered a French trawler and made their way back across the Channel.

The Battle of France had cost Germany more than 27,000 men killed, and around 111,000 wounded. France had lost 92,000 men killed, 200,000 wounded and a staggering 1,800,000 men captured. British casualties amounted to 68,000 killed, wounded and missing, which included those taken prisoner. As the dust was settling in the railway siding at Compiègne, few of either the French or German generals seriously believed that with France now out of the war Britain could continue to fight on alone for anything more than a few weeks. She had left behind on the beaches on Dunkirk and in the lanes and byways of France almost everything she possessed in terms of military equipment. Most British soldiers had returned with nothing more than a rifle. Many had even abandoned these (something unthinkable in a previous age). Tanks, trucks, motor cycles and an astonishing array of civilian vehicles lay abandoned in and around the town. In the weeks following the Armistice with France, German soldiers looked on agog at the scenes of destruction, and posed as tourists in one famous piece of German home-movie footage in front of the bullet-riddled sign DUNKERQUE outside of the town.

However, one thing the British had escaped with intact from Dunkirk was their morale. The national effort involved in rescuing so many men, the harrowing scenes as train after train pulled into stations full of dirty, weary and often wounded men, had galvanised the British people in a way that so far nothing else in the Second World War had managed to do. With Churchill at their head, and with Dunkirk behind them, they came to believe that they could and would fight on against Hitler, with allies or alone if necessary. Even His Majesty King George VI famously commented that he felt a lot happier now that we did not have allies to be polite to. Thus the myth of Dunkirk was born.

Chapter 5

Into Captivity

Life as a prisoner of war holds many hardships that the soldier ordinarily may not have to face. The physical conditions in which captives are held – shelter (or lack of it), and food (or lack of it) – all contribute to the prisoner's daily battle for survival. These have an impact on the soldier's physical health, but then there are factors that affect his mental and emotional well-being also. There is often little or no privacy. There may be long periods of boredom, or conversely prisoners may be worked literally to death. To be held a prisoner of war is in many ways worse than being an ordinary prisoner in a civil prison, for the soldier has committed no crime and yet he is deprived of his liberty. Unlike the civil prisoner his captivity is indefinite; he has no idea if it will be months or even years before he is released. He may even wonder if he will ever be released as his guards hold the power of life and death over him. His best hope may be if his captors see value in him as a bargaining chip, for the prisoner of war is as much as anything else a hostage. Depending on the progress of the war his value – and therefore the standard of his treatment – may increase or decrease. He is deprived of the support of his family and friends who would ordinarily be allowed to visit a prisoner in a civil jail, though if he is lucky he may develop a network of support through close friendships with other prisoners.

All of these challenges were about to be faced by the men of the 2nd/5th Leicesters who now found themselves in enemy hands. The story of 'the men behind the wire' is a part of the Dunkirk legend that is seldom told, for although 300,000 or more men were rescued from the beaches, some 26,000 others fell into German hands. They were left behind to fight their own private war against the Germans, a war of small but meaningful victories over their captors, in which the ultimate prize was defined by only one thing – survival. The prisoner of war experience is deeply engrained in the British psyche. A whole series of feature films based around these ordeals, among them *The Captive Heart* released as early as 1946, *The Wooden Horse* (1950) and the most famous of all *The Great Escape* (1963), have ensured that post-war generations are familiar with these experiences, their terminology and their imagery of barbed wire fences and watch-towers, albeit at the expense of perpetuating some of the clichés associated with them, such as the *Boy's Own* attitudes to POW life and to escaping.

Fortunately, at the end of the war when these men were repatriated, they were debriefed by a special arm of the security services. Today we are familiar with the intelligence agencies MI5 and MI6, but during the Second World War other agencies were established including MI9, which was set up with the objective of monitoring activities in German prisoner of war camps, and to help men to escape or avoid capture in the first place. MI9 produced counterfeit currency and other escape wares and smuggled these into camps. At the end of the war its staff were anxious to debrief POWs, in part at least to assess how effective their own activities had been, and most former prisoners completed a confidential report. Today these are to be found at the National Archives under WO344 and they provide an invaluable resource for historians trying to reconstruct the daily lives of British POWs.

For the men of the 2nd/5th Leicesters who became prisoners this chapter of their lives really began in the immediate aftermath of the fighting, when the gunfire and shelling around Pont a Vendin drew to a close. At first many POWs, having been disarmed and roughly handled by the Germans, were naturally very apprehensive about what would happen to them next. Private Don French remembered: 'I didn't know what to think at first, in fact I was quite concerned!'[1]

Private Maurice Jennings had been shot in the hand in the fighting on the canal bank, but for him no medical attention was available. Faced with over-whelming numbers of British and French prisoners of war, the Germans were unable or unwilling to deal with them, and there were many cases of mis-treatment through neglect. Jennings remembered:

We were in Belgium for five days and four nights in open fields without anything to eat or drink and without any medical attention. I was afraid I might lose my hand. Fortunately, gangrene didn't set in. I palled up with a fellow from Manchester. He had been wounded in the head. There were some trucks on the road that ran by the field and he gave me a nudge to try and jump on a truck when the time came to move out. We succeeded, so we didn't have to march. These trucks took us to a train station. There were some Sisters of Mercy there who attended to my hand and gave us something to eat and drink. The German wounded had also been taken to the station and were loaded on to separate carriages from the POWs.[2]

French remembered they were all, even those who were not wounded, tired, cold and demoralised:

> We were wet through, there had been a thunderstorm, raining all night, everyone was soaked through. They took me to a dressing station, they cut the bandage from your trousers [First Field Dressing] and they put a tissue paper bandage on me. They took all the British bandages and put these here 1917 tissue paper things on. They put us in the square, and we lay there all day. Hundreds there were, all of them wounded. At night they came along with no end of ambulances and took us all away. They put nine of us in each, three on each side and three in the middle.
>
> They set off, and we got in an air raid. All these Jerry drivers pulled in under some trees, out of the way, and they cleared off. They came back about two hours later, after the bombing had stopped. Everything was rocking & shaking with this bombing! Anyway they came back, started the engines again, and we were off on this road again.[3]

He was then taken to an abandoned hospital with no glass in the windows or running water. French staff unloaded the ambulances. The French personnel had either volunteered or had been coerced into remaining at the hospital, and this caused some confusion among the British wounded as to whether they were in fact being repatriated. The following day medics operated to remove the bullet from Don French's shoulder. Conditions were basic to say the least but he remained there for a week to recuperate from the operation. He remembered:

> In the hospital, they'd got no water, when we'd had the operation, you used to have an old tin, you know [with a handle] for a cup. They used to come down the line giving out 'vin blon' or 'vin roug', in a bucket, you dipped your tin in and depending on how far down the line you were you got a full tin or not![4]

After a week he was strong enough to be moved to a POW camp:

> They took us and put us in an old brick factory for a day or two, till they'd got enough to take us to the prisoner of war camp. We weren't really guarded – we couldn't get out of this factory any way! We used to see the Jerries about three times a day, they used to come around. We were there about a week, then we were on our way to Germany on lorries. Well, we thought we were going to Germany anyway. We were somewhere in Germany at one point, but we went to Danzig in Poland.[5]

French, it seems, was one of the luckier ones. Private Horace Greasley and others meanwhile were not so fortunate. A short time after capture, Greasley found himself along with perhaps a thousand other captives, British and French, in a medieval town square. Some had been wounded. All were demoralised, and their beds for the night consisted of the damp stone pavé of the square. Food was not forthcoming from the Germans, and his only meal consisted of some bread stolen from the French. For Greasley and his fellows there were no trucks. The next day the pitiable crowd of humanity began its hungry march eastwards, the column of POWs stretching for at least 3 miles into the distance along tree-lined French roads. For three days and nights they marched, sleeping in fields at night and eating what they could find or scrounge. It was not uncommon for POWs to risk a beating with a rifle butt for leaving the column to try to grab a raw vegetable from the fields as they passed. Bob Monk was also among the weary column of marchers. On one occasion as he marched, he came upon a bundle of postcards filled out by prisoners to inform their next of kin they had been captured. These had apparently been dumped in a ditch by the Germans, perhaps one reason why it took such a long time for news of the captives to reach their loved ones at home. At length, the men on the march reached a railhead and they, like Don French, entrained for the Fatherland.

Battered and beaten they might have been, but the British POWs still possessed a sense of defiance which would help them get through the coming years. Horace Greasley remembered that as there were no toilet facilities in the cattle trucks in which the Germans loaded them, the POWs simply threw whatever they produced out through the slats – preferably when they were passing through a station crowded with German soldiers and civilians. Private Joe White remembered as they reached Germany, their captors demanded that the Tommies hand over their tin helmets (presumably for raw materials for the German war effort). Almost to a man the British prisoners chose instead to hurl them into the Rhine, to the impotent fury of their captors.

Almost all of the Leicestershire regiment soldiers captured in May 1940 were dispatched to prisoner of war camps in German-occupied Poland. Each one was known as a Stalag (an abbreviation of the German Stammlager – base camp), and numbered after the German military district in which it was situated. The vast majority of those Leicestershire regiment men captured in the Dunkirk campaign were sent to Stalag XXA at Thorn, with some sent to Stalag XXIB at Schubin, and others to Stalag XXID at Posen.

Thorn was a fortified town on the River Vistula, ringed by a number of forts. The forts, dark and dank with subterranean vaults and passages, had originally been built by Prussia in the late nineteenth century to defend her eastern border against Russia. The forts provided the basis for the prisoner of war camp, each one being converted into a prison block. The first inmates of the camp were Poles captured in the 1939 campaign. By 1940 these men had largely been released, and as large numbers of British prisoners of war captured in the 1940 campaign fell into German hands, they began to take their places. The British prisoners, who had lost most of their kit when captured in France, were re-equipped by the Germans, often with items of uniform taken from the captured Poles. Photographs of British prisoners often show them wearing a motley selection of greatcoats and soft-peaked Polish caps. In place of boots they were also often issued with wooden clogs which took more than a little getting used to, particularly as they tended to be worn with the foot wrapped in flannel rather than in a sock. Finally, they were issued with a rectangular zinc identity tag which bore their prisoner number. In common with German Army practice, the tag was perforated along the centre line, with the information repeated on both halves, the theory being that if the prisoner died the tag would be broken in half, one half would remain with the prisoner's body and the other half returned to central records. Don French remembered:

> From Danzig we went to camp XXA at Thorn in Poland. They had seven or eight camps there with about a thousand in each. We had ordinary tents to start with. Of course when you get to about November time, there was a lot of frost and snow about. In fact I reckon it was a lot warmer with the snow on the tents than it was with nothing on them!
>
> They were long days they were. Nowt to do and all day to do it in! I couldn't do any work to start with because of my arm, but others they'd captured did. I did get a bit better and to start with I went smashing stones up, to make a road, you used to take about fifty, and a hammer and start smashing them up, but after a while they took us out of that.[6]

At its peak, Stalag XXA held some 20,000 men and administered a number of sub camps or working camps in the immediate area. Prisoners on first arrival at the camp would be assigned to one of the forts, and then subsequently allocated to one of the working camps for duty. The work was varied but included labouring in factories, quarries and on construction of new homes for the Germans the Third Reich wished to resettle in the former Polish territories. It was not uncommon for 12-hour shifts to be worked and the

German Reich ruthlessly exploited the British prisoners almost as a slave labour force.

Private George Arlott was destined to be incarcerated in Stalag XXIB at Schubin, some 30 miles north-east of Posen and about 10 miles west of Thorn. He remembered:

> [After we were captured] we were taken to Arras, which was a transit camp. Then we were put on a train for Poland, we were rammed into these carriages which were really cattle trucks, with just a slot for the window, and we were put in a siding and left all night, no amenities, we had to do all our business in the open. After that we were transported straight through to Poland. [We were allowed off] when we arrived by these barbed wire enclosures, and inside was a cookhouse and so on ...[7]

After a three-day journey across Germany in cattle trucks, Horace Greasley and the POWs with him detrained at a holding camp somewhere in eastern Germany, before continuing their rail journey to Posen, known in Polish as Poznan, in the German-occupied territories in the east. His home that winter of 1940 was to be Stalag XXID at Posen. Like Thorn, Posen was a fortified town, the defences of which were constructed by Prussia in the 1860s as a shield against Russia. The town was ringed by crumbling brick-built forts, two of which, Fort Rauch and Fort VIII (Grolman), made up Stalag XXID. Greasley remembered:

> Fort Eight at Posen had been an old First World War cavalry barracks. The prisoners slept in what was once the stables set aside for the horses. The stables were filled with straw. There were no bunks, no blankets.
>
> The forts, for defence against artillery, were two-thirds underground, with the roof turfed with rough grass. Horses had been stabled on the ground floor, now the sleeping quarters of the Allied POWs. The next level up, effectively still underground, had been the sleeping quarters and the offices of the cavalry, and now housed the German guards ... the level above ground was a series of individual outbuildings, offices and private dormitories for the officers.[8]

The only bedding available to the men was filthy straw, alive with vermin. As the winter of 1940/41 drew on, conditions for the POWs sleeping five to a stall in the former stables were grim, with meagre rations to help them keep out the cold – weak cabbage soup was often the order of the day, Greasley remembered. January of 1941 was particularly bleak. The temperature in

Poland at this time of year can reach −20°C, and it was not uncommon for the men after parading for roll call to be lightly dusted with snow. Greasley testified in his MI9 report that he was hospitalised for eight weeks with diphtheria, which was attributed to the foul conditions in the filthy barracks there, though he conceded that the medical treatment that he received from the Germans was adequate.

Shortly after arriving in the camp, the Germans had paraded the men to establish what their civilian trades had been and to allocate them employment. Arlott remembered:

> I remember we were put on parade and they wanted to know who was a doctor, and who was a farmer and so on . . . well I put my hand up and said I was a farmer, because I'd got no trade, and so they separated the farmers from the rest, and we were marched, through the streets, to a farmer, well they showed us to the farm house, and we had a good meal, first time we'd eaten since we'd been took [prisoner] . . . I know we had potatoes.[9]

Greasley, as a hairdresser, naturally enough was selected to become camp barber. In this he was fortunate as the role meant that he was exempted from the normal working parties that left the camp regularly for labouring duties. The standard cut for most men was a close shave of the head in order to prevent lice. Bob Monk, in common with a lot of other men, claimed that he had been a cook in civil life, reasoning that this would place him in closer proximity to food. The Germans however were suspicious of the large number of men claiming to have culinary skills, and it was soon established that in fact Monk was an apprentice carpenter. His skills were put to use working on building sites in Danzig. In later years he returned there and was able to identify a number of buildings upon which he had worked.

Silesia, in what is now western Poland, was at this time one of the main coal-producing regions of Germany and numbers of British POWs were put to work mining coal. Generally this was regarded by British POWs as the worst type of work – it was hard, dirty and dangerous. Maurice Jennings, after a spell in hospital whilst his hand healed, was in September 1940 posted to the E72 working camp at Beuthen (modern-day Bytom), where he was to spend the next two-and-a-half years as a coal miner at the massive Hohenzollern Mine. Here the British POWs worked alongside Polish civilian workers. Generally speaking, the Polish or German workers cut the coal, whilst the British prisoners acted as labourers for them. Most coal mines ran on three 8-hour shifts per day. In spite of the exhausting nature of the work, those prisoners working the mines received no extra rations. Illnesses were commonplace among these men. In February 1943 Maurice Jennings developed nephritis, an inflammation of the kidneys. The infection is caused by overwork and poor diet, and in May 1943 Jennings was transferred to other, lighter, work at a stone quarry.

Food and work were inextricably linked for the POWs, who were left in no doubt that no work equalled no food. Unlike the enlisted men, NCOs were not obliged to undertake manual labour but here again German interpretation of the rules regarding treatment of prisoners of war was suspect. Corporal Dick Vincent was in a work camp at Bromberg between April 1941 and August 1942 working in a gravel pit. After the war in his MI9 debrief he drew attention to what he saw as the: 'Failure of the detaining power (Germany) to make known the Geneva Convention in regard to the rights of an NCO ie forcing NCOs to work.'[10] In fact, this was something of a grey area as the Geneva Convention actually prohibited the use of senior NCOs for labour in anything other than a supervisory category. Vincent as a corporal, in German eyes, can hardly have been anything other than a junior NCO, given that the equivalent of second lieutenant in the German Army was a non-commissioned rank. Company Sergeant Major Arthur Chambers, who had been captured with his company commander Captain Sidney Brown, was also sent to work at a coal mine, this time at Sosnowice as part of the E538 working party. Chambers was a coal miner in civilian life. However, as a senior NCO he was not expected to work himself but instead his job was to supervise other POWs. This must at times have placed him in a difficult position in relation to his fellow POWs, as effectively he was now an instrument of the Germans.

Rations for men undertaking hard physical labour were desperately poor, and contained hardly enough calories to sustain a man even without manual work, but British prisoners of war in Germany where food was in short supply anyway were low down in the pecking order. The Geneva Convention required the Germans to feed POWs to the same standards as their own soldiers, but there is no doubt that POWs ranked behind the German military first and foremost and the German civil population behind them. As the war progressed, the food situation became much worse, and the only way that the POWs survived was through the Red Cross parcels that reached them from home. Company Sergeant Major Andrew Croxall, who was in Stalag XXA, writing in his MI9 debrief in 1945 added: 'German food rations both at main Stalags and working camps were very bad. Had it not been for the Red Cross food parcels 75% [of us] would have gone under.'[11]

Bob Monk remembered in particular the cans of condensed milk that came with the parcels as adding a vital element of sweetness to the prisoners' otherwise drab diet. Phil Haywood's wife included a butterfly can opener in one of her parcels – a simple thing but it was a godsend to her husband as no one else among his comrades had one. The other main means for the POWs to survive was on food that was supplied to them by the Polish civilian population among which they lived whilst on working parties. There was undoubtedly a great deal of sympathy felt towards the British prisoners of war by the Polish people among whom they lived. Phil Haywood was in no doubt that if it were not for the help that the British received from the Poles (who it should be remembered were on the edge of starvation themselves) then many more would certainly have died. George Arlott remembered: 'We were put to [work] scything – with the harvest. That was the only farm I was on ... it was one German guard to twenty prisoners of war. We basically stole to eat. We stole a chicken egg or whatever ... The Polish people bent over backwards to help us. They treated us very well.'[12]

Private Gordon Chaplin remembered that the food consisted chiefly of potato water and sugar beet. Often the POWs were so hungry that they would eat the root crops from the fields they were sent to tend, straight from the ground and raw. Chaplin grew weaker and weaker and developed jaundice, but was helped by a Polish woman who somehow managed to smuggle some sugar and jam to him. Small wonder then that so many British ex-POWs felt a lifelong debt of gratitude towards the Polish people, who had done so much at such great risk to themselves to help the Allied soldiers in their midst.

Don French returned home in 1945 as skin and bone; it took him many weeks to regain the 2 stones in weight that he had lost as a POW. He recalled:

Food wise, it did dwindle as the war went on but then there wasn't much to start with! You had five to a loaf, and they were only little loaves ... it was brown bread, or brown coloured, and you got a tin or a cup of coffee, or it was supposed to be coffee, ersatz coffee it were. Burnt corn or something they said it were, I don't know! It used to make it brown anyway! You only got two meals a day, odd times you got three. [They] never gave any breakfast in a morning, you didn't get nowt till dinner time, a plate of stew or thin gravy, water, and you got a cup of coffee, and your fifth of a loaf at tea time. Some chaps used to save a bit, [and] somebody else would pinch it – you'd got to eat it, or somebody else would eat it for you! There was quite a lot of that.[13]

The best years for Don French were from about 1942 to 1944, when the POWs from Stalag XXA were dispersed to provide labour on Polish farms. He remembered:

I went out on a farm. Twenty of us went out on a farm the farmers were Poles turned Germans. We ploughed, with a horse, cut the grass, did a bit of sileing [?]. The only thing I didn't like was picking spuds, you used to stand on one and press it in the ground while you picked another up! You only picked half of them up! ...

We used to take the milk at the end, because they'd called the Jerries up that were in charge of the farm ... then we had to take the milk on a horse & cart in the morning, the milk ride they called it. It used to be a two-and-a-half hours job ... We were on this farm when [we heard] the war [was ending]. We didn't have any Jerries with us. You could see your mate on the next farm very often, where the field joined, or perhaps you wouldn't see nobody all day. We got on alright farming, we got four meals a day there.[14]

Leonard Bingley was also held in Stalag XXA, and like French was working on a farm. His diary for that year, 1942, reveals a great deal about the daily battles (and monotony) of POW life. A typical section from autumn 1942 reads as follows:

27 September <u>Sun</u> no work. Breakfast Bacon & Egg. Wrote PC to Dais. Supposed not to be sent before Oct 9.

28 September <u>Mon</u> Spud packing. Weather turned very warm. Did not do much.

29 September <u>Tues</u> Spuds again but cushy job sorting them out on wagon.

30 September <u>Wed</u> Spuds and hot weather what a combination. Still on cushy job.

1 October <u>Thurs</u> Spuds. Same as yesterday. No mail or parcels.

2 October <u>Fri</u> Spuds sorting! No mail or parcels.

3 October <u>Sat</u> As per usual SPUDS!!![15]

Later that month Bingley had moved on to sugar beet, apparently on the same farm:

25 October Sun Work again. Sugar beet. Knocked off 4.00pm Red Cross [parcel] today. PC Dais & Mam.

26 October Mon Sugar beet Finished 12 o'clock. Nice row about it. Parcels up. None for me.

27 October Tues Sugar beet carrying no escort. Thrashing after dinner. Row with Leyer [presumably the farm owner] because we would not work after 6.00.

28 October Wed Escort again. Could not do it. Far too much. Threatened not to do any more.

29 October Thurs Carrying beet. Finished about 3.00pm. Queer rumour about being home early 1943.

30 October Fri Still hot. Finished about 4.15pm. Two new guards.

31 October Sat Change today. Station loading flax. Cushy. Finished 3.30pm. Parcel & 100 [cigarettes].

1 November Sun No work !!! Football match. England 1 Colonies 0. Letter to Dais. PC to Mam.[16]

To some extent, the POWs appear to have been able to negotiate with the farm owner or overseer the amount and rate of work that they were expected to accomplish. On this farm at least, they seem to have been at least reasonably well fed and were hardly the slave labourers depicted in some books on British POW life.

Overall, however, one is struck by how different the war experience of the men captured in the Dunkirk campaign must have been from that of those who were evacuated. Thousands of miles from home, in a strange country which few of the men can have had any knowledge of prior to the war, and forced to work for a sometimes arbitrary and unpredictable enemy regime, these men required particular resourcefulness and a degree of emotional and mental resilience if they were to survive. The elements upon which the prisoners relied for support in these areas will be examined in greater detail in the next chapter.

Chapter 6

Hope and Freedom

For many of the British prisoners of war incarcerated in Poland for five years following the fall of France life was undoubtedly hard, but the men found their own ways of tolerating the conditions, their own support networks and their own ways to enliven the monotony. The guards were the enemy, and survival as a prisoner was often about small victories, but as the years rolled on towards 1945 the balance of power between prisoners and guards began to shift somewhat. The guards were still the ones with the guns, but increasingly they were as trapped in their circumstances as the men they guarded, and the prisoners could see this. Ironically, in the final months of the war, as the Third Reich crumbled in the face of the onslaught from the Red Army in the east, and release and freedom began to appear a distinct possibility at last, the prisoners (and their guards) found themselves in circumstances more dangerous than at any time since they were first captured.

Throughout the chain of prisoner of war camps established by the Germans in western Poland, there were innumerable camp theatre troupes and orchestras. Phil Haywood played the clarinet and was a member of an orchestra in Stalag XXA, but even a single camp such has this had more than one dance band operating at the same time. Haywood's friend Gordon Chaplin sent home a request for a piano accordion. His family sent one to him, through the Red Cross. It travelled via Switzerland and took months to arrive, but amazingly reached him intact. The musical and theatrical life of the camps was incredibly rich and varied and must have provided a distraction from the everyday reality of their situation for a good many POWs. Many men became involved in the theatre which at Stalag XXA was organised by the British actor Sam Kydd, who had been captured in France in 1940. Kydd would go on to become a household name in Britain in the 1960s and 1970s, appearing in *Crossroads*, *Coronation Street*, *Steptoe & Son* and a host of other roles. Kydd was offered the chance of repatriation in 1943 but chose instead to stay as a prisoner of war, so important did he feel his work to be. It was said that the make-believe world of the theatre into which many men entered quite literally kept them sane, for even those who did not have the required talent for acting or singing could find a focus in the construction of sets or the making of costumes from whatever scraps were to hand. Bob Monk's family remember him as a man who could turn his hand to anything and who was particularly ingenious in creating theatre props from whatever he could lay his hands on.

Sporting fixtures were another means of filling the day, and boxing was a popular pastime. Few people today, however, realise either the extent or the importance to morale of football in German prisoner of war camps in the Second World War. With so many prisoners from different regions it was possible to organise leagues and even to hold international matches. Don French remembered: 'When you got out there on these farms, I mean there were hundreds of [POWs], in fact we used to have football teams, and we used to play Sunday afternoons, we used to ride on a horse and cart to the next village to play.'[1] It was even said that the Germans really did try to organise a Germany versus POWs football match for propaganda purposes, as is depicted in the fictional film *Escape to Victory* (1981). The plan was scuppered by the POWs who would not co-operate, though the Germans did get as far as sending a radio broadcast unit to cover the match.

Mail from home was another crucial factor in maintaining prisoners' moral. French recalled: 'We were all nationalities, British, some New Zealanders, Aussies, a few froggies. We'd got a sergeant major in charge of us. Mail wasn't too bad once it got going but it was a long time before you got one to start with to send home. It was about a month old when you got it.'[2]

Private Joe White, it will be remembered, had been captured in the fighting on the canal bank near Pont a Vendin. A remarkable series of letters survive from Joe to his widowed mother, Mrs K.C. White of 22 Underhill Street, Leicester, and these make a fascinating record of his captivity as well as an insight into the life of a prisoner of war. On 3 May 1941, he writes to his mother to tell her that his camp address has now changed from Stalag XXIB to Stalag XXID. He wishes her a happy birthday, and hopes to be with her on her birthday the following year. On 9 November 1941 he writes, this time from Stalag VIIIB at Lamsdorf:

Well mother Dear once again I write to let you know I am alright and feeling fine. I hope you and all at home are the same I got your letter you sent on 16 Sep telling me to write and let you know what I want for Xmas. I would like socks a pullover and shirts, pants, soaps, toothbrush and paste, comb, hairbrush. I do not think you will get this letter till after

Xmas but it will do for when you send another parcel. Well mother Dear how is work coming along? Do not make yourself ill with it. Give my love to Cath and her mother tell them I think of them every day and long to be with them again. Tell Cath to send me some photos please and write and tell me where she works and what she does. I have written to Chas. We get four cards and two letters every four weeks now, so I can write more often now. Well dear I must close now, with all my love and kisses to you all at home, and keep smiling.

From your loving son Joe.[3]

Don French was among the lucky ones as his sweetheart Daisy remained loyal to him during the five long years that they were apart whilst he was held a prisoner. They married upon his return from captivity, but many romances and even marriages did not survive the long years of enforced separation, with only infrequent and out-of-date letters to hold a couple together. By the time Joe White writes to his mother again on 13 December 1942, like so many other prisoners of war he has clearly received a 'Dear John' letter from his sweetheart Cath. His highly touching letter scarcely disguises the fact that he is trying his best to put a brave face on things:

Dear Mum,
This week I received a letter from you and one from Chas and one from a girl at work. I am quite well and feeling fine, I hope you are the same and not worrying about me. Do not upset yourself about what Cath has done. I am not worried about her, I lived 19 years before I met her, I am sure I can live without her again, what do you say? I have seen a lot of trouble these last three years, and a bit more does not make much difference now. I will still come home smiling and have a good time with all my friends. Give my love to Chas, Lily and Janice, I am hoping to see you all again and have a real good party. I am glad Mrs Streathers is writing to me, I would like to know how Charlie is getting on and where he is. I had a Xmas card from the Bishop of Leicester, it was very nice too. I have found out that a boy's best friend is his mother, and I have the best mother in the world to come home to, you are better than all the girls in the world, may God Bless you Dear. I am quite well and healthy working in the open air. There is nothing like a stone quarry to keep you fit, I weigh 11 stone, don't you think that's good. Well I must close now space is getting very short. Give my best regards to all around.

Hope to see you soon, your loving son Joe.[4]

In fact, so many other men had received 'Dear John' letters in this camp that there was actually a club of that name. Joe was inducted into the club with much mock pomp and ceremony. Sadly, Joe was to receive further heart-breaking news whilst he was a prisoner. Another letter in this fascinating series was sent via the Red Cross to the 'British Man of Confidence' or Camp Leader, Stalag 344 Lamsdorf. Dated 26 September 1944, it reads:

> Dear Camp Leader
> I have just received a letter from the British Red Cross Society, London, which contains a very sad message for POW Nr 4190 J. White. Below is a copy of the letter and I ask you to break the news to White in the most suitable manner:
>
> Private J. White POW Nr 4190
> We have been asked by Corporal Charles White, brother of the above mentioned prisoner of war, to arrange for the news to be broken to him of his mother's death on May 22nd. Corporal White's account of the circumstances is as follows:
>
>> 'My mother has been ill since November 1943, but only 6 weeks ago the doctor sent her to the Royal infirmary for an X-Ray. She was taken to Hillcrest Hospital about a month ago. I visited her there … before she died she mentioned my brother's name.'
>
> Please express to Pte White my own deep sympathy in his loss.[5]

There was much mutual support derived from other POWs at times like this, but in the end, as Don French observed, morale was a personal thing, derived from the individual's own personal reaction to his circumstances: 'Morale wasn't too bad. Some were worse than others. Some of us could stick it, some of us couldn't. It was down to you really.'[6] One very important thought above all others, however, kept the POWs going, and this was the hope of eventual Allied victory: 'We did always say we were going to win.'[7]

It was generally agreed that the older guards behaved reasonably towards the POWs, presumably because having lived through the First World War, they were aware that the fortunes of war can quickly change and the boot might soon be on the other foot. Younger guards, however, who had in all likelihood grown up knowing nothing but Nazi ideology and who were full of certainty about the superiority of the 'master race' were frequently described by ex-POWs as bastards. Don French remembered: 'The Germans weren't too bad.

Mind you if you were doing something wrong and they saw you and they let fly at you, they would do. That only happened once or twice.'[8]

In fact, French himself was the victim of German brutality, when he was bayoneted in the leg by a German guard because he did not stand up fast enough when ordered to do so. Horace Greasley likewise had a confrontation with a German guard who came into his barber's shop in the camp, demanding to be shaved ahead of the British prisoners who were already waiting. Greasley made the mistake of insulting the German, not realising he spoke English, and received a severe beating as a result. George Arlott had this to say on the subject:

> [The guards] were mostly Wehrmacht, ordinary German soldiers, and we heard all about the SS, they told us to keep out of their way, as they are brutal with you ... The Wehrmacht treated us fairly. They were the best of the Germans from our point of view. I'm afraid they didn't treat other people as well as they treated us. They were very brutal with the Jews ... I saw it ... you've got to realise that the Polish winters are bloody cold – freezing – it was nothing to see a truckload of Jews who were in a camp near where we were, loaded into lorries and driven round, until they were stiff.[9]

The Germans at least allowed the British POWs to develop the sense of community and mutual support that was essential if they were to survive their ordeal. Leonard Bingley wrote in his diary for Christmas Eve, 24 December 1943: 'Knocked off 12 noon. Had a hell of a good time at night, bags of beer & schnapps, sing song & dance. Lots to eat.'[10] The following day he wrote: 'Xmas Day again. May God Bless all my loved ones. Lovely set out dinner. 5 courses. Real lovely. Bags of drink and fun.'[11]

Despite the image portrayed by Hollywood films, in particular *The Great Escape*, escaping from a prisoner of war camp in occupied Poland was, for most of the British other ranks, a practical impossibility. They simply did not have the material resources to do this. They had little free time on their hands, often working a six-day week, they were weak and often underfed, they had no money, they had no means of producing forged documents and they had no access to civilian clothes and so would have stood out anywhere as POWs. Above all, most of them had no foreign-language skills. Escaping was largely the preserve of officers, who did not have to work and who had the time and opportunity to devise such schemes.

However, there is evidence that more than one soldier from the 2nd/5th battalion did at least try to escape. Private Gordon Chaplin, who had originally been captured the day after the Germans broke through the Canal Line in France, had been incarcerated at Stalag XXA at Thorn in June of 1940. In 1941 he was transferred to Stalag XXB at Marienburg (Malbork in modern Poland). He had first tried to make it back to England in 1941 whilst with a working party in nearby Danzig (Gdansk), but was recaptured in the city by the Germans. He was, perhaps, hoping to board a ship heading for neutral Sweden, and this may have been a spur of the moment opportunist escape, for he does not appear to have been at large for any length of time before recapture. On the second occasion, in January 1944, he was working at a malt factory in Marienwerder, now known as Kwidzyn in northern Poland, but formerly a German city in East Prussia. On this occasion, according to his MI9 statement made on repatriation, he escaped with three companions, Herbert Norton of the Grenadier Guards, a man named Mitchell from the Rifle Brigade and Sid Smith of the Leicesters (probably 4857473 Private S. Smith). This escape appears to have involved more planning. It is possible that at this late stage in the war they may have been aware of the close proximity of the advancing Red Army and may have been trying to reach Soviet lines – if so, this was a risky strategy. According to the statement, he was at large for two months before recapture in March of 1944. After this he was sent to a punishment camp at Reisenburg (Proibuty in modern Poland).[12]

In July of 1941, Horace Greasley and many of his comrades were transferred by German Army truck to Saubsdorf in the Sudetenland area, on what was known as working party E166. Saubsdorf was a sub camp of Stalag 344 at Lamsdorf, which itself was the re-numbered former Stalag VIIIB. Lamsdorf had a long history of use as a detention centre – there had been a camp for POWs here in the Franco-Prussian war of 1870–71 – and the first barrack blocks to be occupied by POWs in the Second World War were in fact originally built to hold British and French prisoners in the First World War. It had a reputation as one of the best-equipped camps in the east, and certainly the medical facilities were of an acceptable standard. Conditions here were a great improvement on Greasley's previous camp; the men were given hot showers, better food and slept in proper bunks with mattresses. Saubsdorf (now known as Supikovice) lies about 2 miles across the Polish border inside the modern Czech Republic. Here they were put to work in a stone quarry, belonging to a German civilian, Herr Rauchbach.

Here Greasley was possibly working alongside Joe White, who was also at this time labouring in a stone quarry attached to Stalag VIIIB. There were no fences around this camp, the men were simply locked in their huts at night. The quarry was situated on the edge of an enormous forest and the Germans clearly felt that this and the 400 miles of occupied territory in every direction was more than enough to deter escape attempts. The only steps the German guards took to prevent the escape of POWs was to remove their boots and trousers at night. Joe White remembered that one winter's night a fire broke out in a lime kiln at the quarry. It quickly spread to the POW huts and the men were forced to run out into the snow with nothing on their nether regions. His feet were badly frostbitten as a result.

Working alongside the POWs were Polish civilian women who earned the respect and gratitude of men like Joe White, as, at great risk to themselves, they often smuggled in extra food for the British, as well as conveying pieces of war news to them. However, Herr Rauchbach himself was also secretly an ardent anti-Nazi, having Jewish ancestry and seeing himself as Silesian rather than German. Rauchbach's daughter Rosa worked in the camp as an interpreter, and she too was an anti-Nazi. Greasley spoke some German, and soon formed a relationship with Rosa Rauchbach. In addition to bringing vital extra rations of rabbits and vegetables to Greasley and the other prisoners, in January 1944 she also began to smuggle radio parts into the camp. Although she would not reveal her sources to the prisoners, it seems likely that she had contacts with the Polish resistance. The clandestine radio and others like it, which were constructed by prisoners in other camps across the Third Reich, were vital in keeping up morale among the prisoners in the second half of the war. Their mail from home was heavily censored, and the Germans fed them an endless diet of lies and propaganda concerning the progress of the war. When the makeshift radios crackled into life they picked up news reports from the BBC, informing the prisoners for the first time of the German defeat at Stalingrad, and the fact that the Germans were being pushed back in the east.

Later that year, the assistance that Greasley was receiving from Rosa Rauchbach reached a new apex. He testified later in his MI9 debrief that: 'In March 1944 [I] discussed with [a] German woman an escape. This person obtained for me travel warrants, ration books, passports [and a] German air force uniform. Her name is Rosa Rauchbach. Owing to [my] detention in Lamsdorf through eye trouble my escape was not possible.'[13]

If escape for many was largely out of the question, the POWs did at least have other options open to them in order to continue the war from inside the camps and to hinder the German war effort. One of these was sabotage of the numerous coal mines, factories and construction projects where they were engaged. Company Sergeant Major Andrew Croxall, who had been captured on 27 May 1940, was sent initially to Stalag XXA at Thorn. In July of that year he was sent as part of a working party to Czersk in East Prussia, about 70 miles south-west of Danzig. Here they were engaged in construction work, particularly road-making and laying sewers. Croxall records in his MI9 questionnaire that while the men were back-filling the trench for the main sewer, they deliberately broke every third or fourth pipe. Joe White and his comrades deliberately damaged a steam locomotive used for hauling wagons full of stone at the quarry in which they worked. Spare parts took months to arrive, but the sabotage backfired on the prisoners, as in the intervening period they were used as human locomotives to haul the wagons!

The German managers of coal mines in occupied Poland were under no illusions about the attitude of British POWs to their work. According to the Auschwitz Museum website, one German manager stated: 'The English deliberately work more slowly, and sometimes state with utter frankness that they have no intention of mining coal that will be converted to aviation fuel and used against their countrymen ...'[14] Direct acts of sabotage, however, were difficult in a coal mine because the prisoners knew that there were usually comrades working at lower levels who would be trapped if they, for example, attempted to block a shaft.

The experience of officers differed considerably from that of other ranks. Most importantly of all, they were not required to work and were held in their own camps, known as Oflags (Offizier-lager). Lieutenant Robert Sharp, who had been captured at the Pont Maudit near Pont a Vendin, was sent initially to Oflag VIIC, which was located at Laufen Castle in south-eastern Bavaria. In the summer of 1940 this camp was filled to capacity and beyond with British officers whom the Germans had captured in France. This overcrowding was the cause of continual complaints to the Red Cross and German authorities by the British officers, and as soon as other accommodation became available they were dispersed.

In September of 1941, Sharp was sent to Oflag VIB at Warburg in Westphalia. This was the scene of the 'Warburg Wire Job' in August 1942. A team of officer POWs constructed a combination ladder and bridge which, after shorting out the camp lights, they threw across the barbed wire fences of the camp, enabling a number of them to escape. It seems unlikely, however, that Sharp was involved in this escape, as for five months at Warburg he was very ill with septic impetigo, which he caught in the shower room. He described conditions at Oflag VIB in the winter of 1941–42 as 'very bad' and the camp as having very poor medical facilities. He also described the German medical officers there as being inefficient.[15]

In October of 1942 Sharp was moved to Oflag VIIB at Eichstatt, Bavaria. A Red Cross report on this camp from November of 1942 reads:

> Oflag VIIB – Hohenfels in S. Bavaria. All the prisoners at this camp were transferred here from Oflag VIB when that camp was closed. The removal was satisfactorily accomplished, and included reserves of provisions, the library, etc., and even the camp cat. It is divided into two sections, called the Upper and Lower Camps. Upper camp consists of barracks arranged on both sides of a small valley. Farther down the valley are five hutments called the Lower Camp.
>
> Between the two are large playing fields, i.e. a football ground and an ice hockey ground, which have been laid out by the prisoners themselves. The officers in the Upper Camp have been permitted to organise their own section. Sanitary installations are said to be entirely adequate and electricity is installed in all the barracks. There are stoves in each room, but fuel has been limited to preserve a good stock for the really cold weather.[16]

Eichstatt was one of the camps selected by the Germans for 'reprisals'. They claimed that following the Dieppe Raid of 1942, an instruction had been found on a dead British soldier to the effect that any captured German soldier was to be handcuffed for security. The Germans seized on this and selected prisoners in certain camps to receive the same treatment, even though they knew it was against the Geneva Convention. In Oflag VIIB 321 officers and 60 other ranks were selected for 'reprisals'. The Red Cross report continued:

> Prisoners who are handcuffed are quartered in Block I of the Upper Camp. The number of these prisoners remains fixed, and if for any reason, such as illness, a prisoner of war is unmanacled, another takes his place. The men are freed from time to time during the day and night. They are able to see and converse with others in the camp. The Camp Leader reports that they have been well treated and receive special kindnesses, such as the use of a larger space for exercise and a higher basic food ration. Their morale is said to be excellent.[17]

In fact, a Major Booth in Oflag VIIB kept a diary detailing this treatment. He confirmed that if a prisoner was sick then another volunteer did indeed take his place in the shackles. The handcuffs went on at 0800 hours and were removed at 2100 hours, with an hour's break at lunchtime. In fact, it became a standing joke in the camp that the handcuffs used by the Germans were so poorly made that any POW who wished was perfectly capable of undoing them, though this was generally not done in front of the guards to avoid antagonising them. Booth concluded that the worst aspect of this treatment was the fact that those undergoing it were kept apart from other prisoners and could not enjoy the shows and other entertainment provided for the majority.

Sharp's own impressions of the camp, however, were less positive. In his POW debrief report for MI9, he describes further reprisals against POWs not mentioned either by Booth or the Red Cross in their reports. These included the removal of mattresses by the Germans and the forcing of prisoners to attend all-night parades. The Red Cross report, meanwhile, continued:

> In the Lower Camp accommodation is not quite so good, lighting is inadequate, only acetylene lamps are provided. Brick stoves provide the heating, but are said to be of better quality than those in the Upper Camp. The orderlies' section was very overcrowded. Sanitary installations are bad. Clothing is fairly satisfactory and Red Cross parcels arrived regularly. Ten British doctors, three dentists and sixteen medical orderlies are in charge of the health of the prisoners.[18]

Sharp also complained about the poor rations throughout the five years that he was a prisoner. However, research shows that the British officers in German hands were generally fed to the same standard as German depot troops, which was in turn better than the food German civilians were receiving at that time. It may be true that British officers, many of whom came from privileged backgrounds, did not fully appreciate that the German people had been on a war footing for some time prior to 1939, and that basic rations in Germany were generally inferior to their English equivalents both in terms of quality and quantity.

Oflag VIIB was the scene of a tragedy, when in the closing days of the war the Germans began to evacuate the camp in the face of advancing American forces. A column of officer POWs on the march were mistakenly bombed by Allied aircraft who took them to be a column of German troops, causing many deaths among men who might reasonably have assumed they were at last close to freedom.

For Greasley and his comrades in the camps in the east, the approaching Red Army in January of 1945 meant not liberation but a forced march in the depths of winter, as their captors sought to evade the advancing Russians. This so-called 'death march' was remembered with horror by many of the POWs who took part in it. Leonard Bingley managed to record what happened in his small pocket diary:

Thursday 18 January: As per usual called in from work at midday. Rumours of moving by marching to Schniedermule.

Friday 19 January: Not moving today. Probably tomorrow. Red Cross bulk issue up and 25 fags.

Saturday 20 January: Started march. Up 3.00am start 7.00am. 25km. Slept in fields. Frozen. Sholitz.

Sunday 21 January: Burnburg after all day march. 40km. Garage bed.

Monday 22 January: Still marching. Its murder. Reached Immenheim about 4.00pm (cow shed).

Tuesday 23 January: Russians overtook us and we are FREE. Dropped a Bollock. Taken by Jerry after 8 hrs freedom. Walked to Vandsberg.

Wednesday 24 January: Stayed all day in a barn.

Thursday 25 January: Left V. and arrived Flatow about 4.00pm. Received 1/3 loaf and sausage.

Friday 26 January: Stayed all day and dragged out at 10.30pm. Snowstorm and sleep.

Saturday 27 January: Arrived at Jastrow in a church. Found some American Red Cross [parcels]. Left at 3.00pm and arrived at a big State farm on Sun.

Sunday January 28: We stayed here all day and received an issue of spuds. Slept in a loft with the Russians [POWs].

Monday 29 January: 9.30am left State farm and arrived at a big Lager about 1.30pm. Good billet EL and fire. Soup and bread.

Tuesday 30 January: Went on to a Barracks at Gr Born. Had good billet and pinched 17 loaves.

Wednesday 31 January: Up at 4.00 and off at 6.00. Went 40km. Hell of a day. Billeted in a barn about 8.00pm at Barwalde.

Thursday 1 February: Off at 10.00pm. Easy walk today to a farm at Bad Polzin about 18km. Got a bit of a Red Cross parcel and a few fags.

Friday 2 February: Made and reached Schwelbein about dusk. Barn again.

Saturday 3 February: ON and ...

Sunday 4 February: ON and ...

Monday 5 February: ON and ...[19]

One might wonder why the Germans went to such lengths to hang on to their prisoners when it might have been thought that they were more trouble than they were worth. However, the endless marches in apparently random directions seem to have had only one purpose: to keep the prisoners out of the hands of the rapidly approaching Russian, American and British armies. We can only conclude that their German captors saw value in the prisoners as possible bargaining chips or even as human shields in the event of a Nazi 'last stand', and tried desperately to cling on to them for as long as possible.

Bingley's remarkable diary simply records the word 'marching', until:

Sunday 18 February: Rest.

Monday 19 February: Still resting. Rumours of staying for a while.

Tuesday 20 February: Resting again. Flogged watch. Officer says making for Schwerin and Lager.

Wednesday 21 February: Off again – did about 15km. Had a good soup and 3 days rations. Bread Marg and Sugar.

Thursday 22 February: Moved about 8.00am. About 20km. Had a fairly good soup. Broke with Tom Ross.

Friday 23 February: Off at 7.30am. Did about 18km. Rumours of resting tomorrow.

Saturday 24 February: Resting today and rations up. Bread – Cheese – Marg. Not too bad now.

Sunday 25 February: Off again. Did about 18km. Had a good supply of spuds and soup. Flogged pullover for bread.

Monday 26 February: Hell of a wet day today. Drizzle all day. Did about 25km. Finished 29km from Schwerin.

Tuesday 27 February: Resting today. Rations up. Bread, Marg and cheese. Rumour of staying here.

Wednesday 28 February: Off again 15km. Rumours of train. Red Cross rations tomorrow. May God grant it is so. [Added later:] But I am afraid it is just a rumour.

Thursday 1 March: New guards take over. 27km through Schwerin. Saw some Red Cross parcels. Rain.

Friday 2 March: Another 18km. Just past Wittenberg. Good billet and food. Staying here.

Saturday 3 March: Eat well today and smoked well. French & Italians left us today.

Sunday 4 March: Stayed here again and had another good day of feeding. Taffy is doing barber and feeding me well. Moving tomorrow.

Monday 5 March: Taffy went by wagon and I dropped a bollock. Got separated and he has all my kit. Only 4km today.

Tuesday 6 March: Staying here a bit. Rations bread, marg, syrup. Deadly here. Feel lost without Taffy.

Wednesday 7 March: It's a rotten place here. Rumours of Red Cross parcels, but we don't get it. May we soon move.

Thursday 8 March: Rations up again. Butter & sugar & Marg. Big air raid last night over Hamburg. They say we may go on Work Parties from here.

Friday 9 March: Moved today to new Coy. About 18km. Still separate from Taffy. Rumours of work from here. Also Red Cross parcels.

Saturday 10 March: Some of the boys went working today and did alright. Supposed to be Red Cross parcels soon. Don't believe it.

Sunday 11 March: Caught for work today until 10.30pm. Red Cross rumours abound but its all balls. We've had 'em.

Monday 12 March: Here today. News at 6.15 was Red Cross parcels. Up at 2.00am with Grainger American and 200 fags between 3. Went in with US chaps.

Tuesday 13 March: Still here. Marked unfit for work. Air raid again. That makes every day for 10 days.

Wednesday 14 March: Still here today. Fed fairly well. Today on potatoes.

Thursday 15 March: Rumours of more Red Cross parcels. About ⅓ of a loaf to make up. Eat well again on spuds.

Friday 16 March: As per usual. Rumours of moving Sat at destination unknown. Wish we could get settled.

Saturday 17 March: Still here and a wet day. Looks like being a hungry one also. Would like to move from here.

Sunday 18 March: Not moving today. Got a few spuds and eggs for today so will be OK. Moving Mon.

Monday 19 March: Got with Taffy and left behind as sick, others moved off maybe dropped B. Yapp behind somewhere.

Tuesday 20 March: Moved off surprise about 20km. Maybe join another column. Rations at 12.30pm. Saw Nedub [?] chap and one from Skempek [?] and one from Sa ... [?]

Wednesday 21 March: Went a good march today about 32km. Bread only. Soup tomorrow. Getting near the Elbe.

Thursday March 22: Crossed the Elbe at DOMITZ after 11km or just over. More columns in vicinity.

Friday 23 March: Staying today. Rumours of two more days. Can we believe it. Had wash down in river. Had restful day.

Saturday 24 March: Up at 4.30am. Soup 6.00am. Off at 7.00am. Not much progress. Big Yank column passed. Tony Coulthard died during night at Kalterhof [?] Domitz. Did about 20km.

Sunday 25 March: Moved about 20km but no Stalag – the lousy Filthy Bastards. Saw air display by the boys.

Monday 26 March: Did about 16km today. Still round the same area. Red Cross parcels rumoured again.

Tuesday 27 March: Stayed today at farm. Red Cross nix. Bread up at breakfast. Out in fields all day grassing [?].

Wednesday 28 March: Still here today. Much colder. Rations included Peach jam OK. Another list of names went in.

Thursday 29 March: Moved off unexpectedly. Did about 24km through wet drizzle most of day. Prop[aganda] says Boys made big airborne landing.

Friday 30 March: About 28km today wet and miserable towards CELLE. God bless Dais, Marg, Billie & Mam.

Saturday 31 March: Moved about 18km and arrived out 1.00pm. Rumours that the ... is handing us over. Resting tomorrow.

Sunday 1 April: Resting today. Wash at a stream. Prop says two more days and finish marching.

Monday 2 April: Off again. About 25km. Rumours stronger than ever about tomorrow being at a camp. Please God it is so.

Tuesday 3 April: Billie's birthday. God Bless and Protect him. Not moved up to 12 o'clock waiting for ½ hour notice. Moving tomorrow.

Wednesday 4 April: Off in the 1st party at 2.00am. Arrived camp and had fine bath and delouse. Camp is a deadly place. Air raid at tea.

Thursday 5 April: This is a working camp!! 42 men to a room. Food is good. It's not too bad after all but we are working tomorrow (LEHRTE). Boys are near here.

Friday 6 April: Out working at a station where the bombs hit. Made a hell of a mess. Our troops are so near we are moving Sat.

Saturday 7 April: Moved off about 8.30am. Bags of our planes about. Air raids and bombing all over and round us. 12km.

Sunday 8 April: March again. 9 to loaf yesterday. Prop is we are surrounded by our boys. Roll on the Boat! Few kms. Prop says hand over in a few days. No rations left.

Monday April 9: Stayed the day. Bags of rumours about re our troops but nothing can be definite. Bread up. Rumours of moving Tues.

Tuesday 10 April: Last night air raids. Today also. Prop says we are surrounded & cannot move. Artillery fire late at night.

Wednesday 11 April: Artillery fire all night. May God grant us a speedy liberation Amen. Forced march at 5.30pm.

Thursday 12 April: Billet at midnight. Marched off again at 7.00am. Billet at 12 o'clock. Decent bed for once. 2 soups per day now, no bread.

Friday 13 April: rice before marching off. Got a fag today. Marched about 15km through woods. Browned off.

Saturday 14 April: Marching through woods – guards left us. FREE!!! Walked to Yankee lines. Bags eats, drinks smokes. Civvy billet W ... [?].

Sunday 15 April: Transported by Yanks. 12 hrs ride to F ... [?] Still bags to eat, drink, smoke. Rumours of flying home.

Monday 16 April: Arrived 1.30am. Billet in a hotel. Bags to eat again and smoke.

Tuesday 17 April: Some of the boys went off today to Hildesheim ... for flying to Blighty. Still bags to go at. Went to Borghorst.

Wednesday 18 April: Still hanging around waiting for transport to airport. Roll on. getting around the town.

Thursday 19 April: Went to airport at Rheine about 2.30pm. Waited all day and returned to camp at 10.00.

Friday 20 April: Airport first thing, went to Brussels in a 4 engined bomber (very sick). Stayed night in Brussels. Good billet and food.

Saturday 21 April: Left Brussels about 5.45pm arrived in Blighty at 6.40pm at Manston near Margate. Thank God for his goodness to us all.

Sunday 22 April: Spent day at camp in Horsham. Fitted up and paid. Good organisation and food. Home tomorrow.

Monday 23 April: Left Horsham 1.50pm. Arrived Waterloo 3.00pm. Caught 4.50pm to Leicester. Home about 8.00pm. Wonderful.[20]

Walter Graves and Joe White were also among the Leicestershire Regiment men who took part in the 'death march' out of Poland and back into Germany. Prisoners of many different nationalities were mixed together and Graves befriended a Russian POW called Petre, a young lad about 18 years old who was very sick and almost on the point of starvation. The German treatment of British POWs was highly civilised in comparison to that meted out to Soviet prisoners, who were frequently left outside in open fields with no shelter, and who were often given no rations whatsoever, leaving them to scrape roots from the ground. Graves shared what food he had with the young Russian and nursed him as much as he could. When the column of sick and starving men reached German soil, SS troops arrived and began to sort out all Soviet POWs who were mixed with the English. Graves begged, stole and borrowed items of British uniform from fellow prisoners and kitted the young Russian out with it, in order to pass him off as a British soldier. The ruse however did not work, as an SS soldier spoke Russian and when questioned the lad gave himself away. He was taken away and shot, whilst Graves tried to intervene but was felled with rifle butts and beaten by his German guards.

On the march westward Joe White and his comrades shared what food they had with Soviet prisoners held alongside them. In gratitude the Russians – who had nothing else – responded with their voices, giving an impromptu Red Army concert in the open air. Joe White had been injured whilst working at the

Private Gordon Chaplin, of Sileby, captured on the road to Dunkirk at La Bassée, 27 May 1940. (*Mrs L. Chaplin*)

Zinc POW ID tag of Corporal Dick Vincent. This type was issued to all British POWs; it bears the man's official German POW number and the name of his camp. (*Mr R. Vincent*)

KR.GEF. LAGER
THORN
Nr: 6 6 1 6

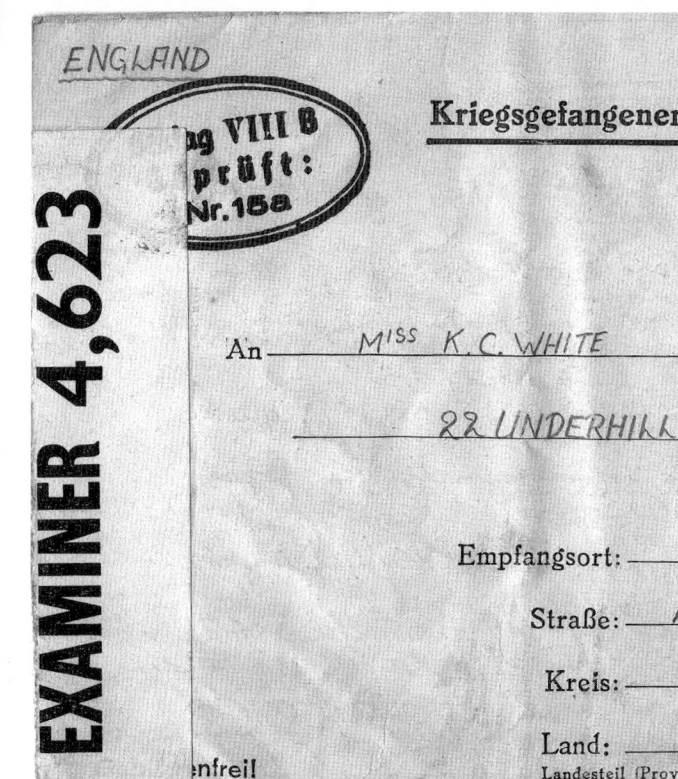

ENGLAND

EXAMINER 4,623

Kriegsgefangenenpost

g VIII B
prüft:
Nr.15a

18.12.42 –14

An———— M^{iss} K.C.WHITE

————— 22 UNDERHILL STREET

Empfangsort: ——— LEICESTER —————

Straße: ——— LEICESTERSHIRE —————

Kreis: ————————————

Land: ——————— ENGLAND

Landesteil (Provinz usw.)

nfrei!

An original letter sent home from a
POW camp by Private Joe White.
(*Author's collection*)

Private Joe White, of Leicester.
He was one of many POWs who
received a 'Dear John' letter
whilst in captivity. (*Mrs J. Lewis*)

Fort XI at Stalag XXA at Thorn, as it appears today. The loop-holed defences are clearly visible. (*PKO photography Poland*)

A modern photograph of the entrance to a prisoners' barracks at Fort VII, Thorn, part of Stalag XXA. The original German barrack number is still visible. (*PKO photography Poland*)

(*Left*) Private Kenneth Callaghan, of Leicester, captured on 26 May 1940 and seen here at Stalag XXA Thorn. (*Author's collection*)

(*Centre*) Private Gordon Chaplin in captivity with his piano accordion. It was sent to him by his family via Switzerland, and amazingly arrived intact many months later. (*Mrs L. Chaplin*)

(*Right*) Private Horace 'Jim' Greasley, a hairdresser from Ibstock. Captured on 26 May 1940, later in the war he helped to smuggle radio parts into a POW camp. (*Mr H. Greasley*)

The entrance to Fort VIII, 'Fort Grolman' at Posen, part of Stalag XXID, as seen today. This view would have been familiar to Horace Greasley and others. (*PKO photography Poland*)

One of several camp orchestras and bands formed in Stalag XXA. (*Mrs J. Haywood*)

Private Maurice Jennings, of Lutterworth. Wounded in the left hand and captured on 26 May 1940, he was later put to work as a prisoner in the enormous Hohenzollern coal mine. (*Mr M. Jennings*)

The Great Hohenzollern coal mine at Beuthen, Upper Silesia (now Bytom in Poland), where many British POWs worked. (*Author's collection*)

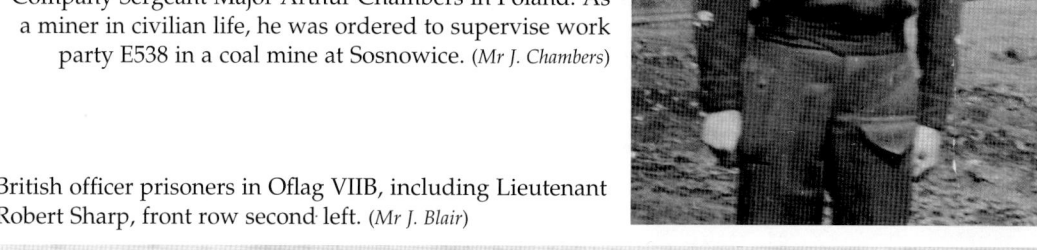

Company Sergeant Major Arthur Chambers in Poland. As a miner in civilian life, he was ordered to supervise work party E538 in a coal mine at Sosnowice. (*Mr J. Chambers*)

British officer prisoners in Oflag VIIB, including Lieutenant Robert Sharp, front row second left. (*Mr J. Blair*)

Company Sergeant Major Andrew Croxall, senior NCO of C Company, 2nd/5th Leicesters. His son, Anthony Croxall, was to be killed in action with the Leicestershire Regiment in 1944. It was a shattering blow from which he never recovered. (*Mr R. Vincent*)

Private Bob Monk, who enlisted in the TA in May 1939 and was captured on the Deule Canal on 26 May 1940. (*Mr J. Monk*)

One of the camp football teams, believed to be in Stalag XXB. Football and boxing were the two main sporting activities in wartime POW camps. (*Mr J. Monk*)

Lance Corporal Leonard Bingley, who spent much of his time as a POW on agricultural work. (*Mrs C. Wheat*)

German POW camp money. Prisoners were paid for their work for the Germans, but in currency that could be used only within the camp. This note was kept as a souvenir by Leonard Bingley. (*Mrs C. Wheat*)

Relatives of Leicestershire prisoners packing POW parcels at Quorn Court, Loughborough. Colonel Craddock, owner of the house, stands at the back. By his left shoulder stands Mrs Joan Haywood, wife of Private Phil Haywood. (*Mrs J. Haywood*)

stone quarry – a slab had fallen from a wagon and broken his leg. The Germans had very quickly found a doctor for him and the leg had been set, but now White walked with some difficulty. Nevertheless, he and a comrade managed to evade their elderly German guard during one of the lengthy marches, and the pair eventually found themselves in Nuremberg in April 1945 as the war was coming to an end. They were present at the parade ground that had been used by the Nazi Party for its pre-war rallies as the Nazi eagle was toppled and the giant swastika ceremonially destroyed by victorious US troops.

Horace Greasley's guards, meanwhile, had led their men away from their camp to an abandoned farmstead. No one was quite sure where they were going, or what the intentions of the guards were. However, with the Russians now closing in fast, the guards had other priorities, and one morning Horace and his comrades woke up to find that their captors had simply vanished. Unsure what to do next, the POWs just carried on walking in the same direction as before. It was not long before they encountered the first Russian patrol. There was much handshaking, the vodka flowed freely and more than a few tears were shed by the British prisoners, overcome by emotion as they realised that their ordeal as captives was finally over. Before long the British soldiers were in a convoy of Red Army trucks heading for Prague. The city was a scene of destruction. The bodies of German soldiers and Czech civilians littered the streets. Other Germans had been strung up from lamp posts by the vengeful Soviet soldiery.

The British prisoners were told it would take a little time to organise transport for so many men. They were given money and allowed to wander the city, but as the days turned to weeks, Greasley and his comrades realised they had exchanged one form of captivity for another. They were now being held as bargaining chips by that supreme gamesman, Josef Stalin, who wanted the return of Soviet prisoners of the Germans who were now in British and American hands. It was June 1945 before the weary British prisoners were finally allowed to leave Prague. Loaded on to Red Army trucks once again, they were eventually taken to an American airbase some 25 miles west of the city. Fresh linen, American cigarettes and beer awaited them. A few days later and Greasley was aboard a converted bomber, heading back over the white cliffs of Dover.[21]

Don French was with a column of POWs who were marched out of Poland and into the northern part of Germany. For them their captivity ended when their march took them into the path of the advancing British forces. By now the Germans had disappeared and abandoned the prisoners of war in a temporary compound, constructed in a field to hold them overnight. French remembered that:

> The Scots Guards cut our wire. They came one Monday morning, and said, 'You're in our area now! We're not going to cut the wire down, as we don't know what will happen', they came back the next week to cut the wire down. We were just in a field with barbed wire round it. When the Scots Guards cut it down we went down to the town, went there and went knocking on doors [to find billets]. We had six chaps in each house.[22]

George Arlott remembered:

[At the end of the war] We were working on the railway, in a railway shed, loading and unloading, manual work, you know, and we were told one morning when we got up to get packed, it was pitch darkness, but we were told we were moving out, and all we could do was get what we could. All we were allowed was an overcoat – I still had my overcoat. And we set off ... The Germans were retreating ... we marched through the snow [and] they used to dump us anywhere, on farmer's land, places like that. [Finally we reached] Nuremberg or Regensberg, [where] the Americans took control.[23]

After a few weeks' leave in which they had the chance to begin to get to know their families once again, Don French, Joe White, Leonard Bingley and other Leicestershire men who had been captured in 1940 were ordered once more to report to military bases in England. Most of the ex-prisoners who had been repatriated were now to be trained for jungle warfare, for their next destination was to be the Far East. With Germany out of the war, attention now shifted to Japan, whose defeat it was envisaged would require every available man. The invasion of Japan was planned for the spring of 1946, but the two atomic bombs dropped in August 1945 brought this campaign abruptly to a close, and the ex-prisoners were then quickly demobilised.

Throughout their five years of captivity, the one thing above all others that really kept the British POWs in Germany going were the parcels that they received. These contributed both to their physical welfare, in as much as they contained vital foodstuffs that could not be obtained by other means, and also to the prisoners' mental well-being. This was because the parcels were a link with home, and reassured the POWs that they had not been forgotten. For example, on 21 March 1942 Leonard Bingley recorded: 'Leicesters parcels distributed. Tin Bovril & Glucose sweets.'[24]

Indeed, almost as soon as news broke of the first local men captured in 1940, the people of Leicestershire mobilised to begin gathering materials and funds to help their loved ones who were now incarcerated in Germany. The *Leicester Mercury* reported that on 11 September 1940, Captain and Mrs L. Nihell-Preau of Quorn held a garden party to raise money for POW comforts, and collected £45 towards the purchase of provisions. The fund-raising events included a dog show and stalls manned by the Girl Guides and Women's Voluntary Service (forerunner of the WRVS). The *Green Tiger*, meanwhile, reported that the regimental Old Comrades Association was making a grant of £8 each month to the Red Cross to provide parcels for prisoners of war.

Leonard Bingley, in his diary for 20 May 1942, records the receipt of a parcel from the Mayoress of Leicester, containing 270 cigarettes and tobacco. There are also a great many other references in his diaries, however, to letters to and from a Mrs German, and this was in fact the wife of Lieutenant Colonel Guy German of the 1st/5th Leicesters. Guy German had been captured in Norway along with a number of his men in April 1940, and Rosemary German was one of the prime movers in organising supplies for the Leicestershire men in captivity. Directly after her husband and his men fell into enemy hands she founded the Leicestershire Prisoners of War Relief Committee. Premises at 13 Baxtergate, Loughborough, were put at her disposal, and the fund that she began to organise on behalf of the prisoners was opened with a £50 donation from the Mayor of Loughborough. As early as 25 September 1940 the *Leicester Mercury* reported that Mrs German's fund to date had raised £2,000. Helpers were busy packing parcels and, with an awareness that winter was fast approaching, the fund had already dispatched 1,800 knitted garments, including socks, mufflers, balaclava helmets and pullovers, and 968 other comforts, including blankets and pyjamas. Later that month the paper reported that Canon Payne and Lady Oliver were also organising parcels for prisoners.

The committee decided to divide the county into areas, and to appoint one of its members to each to act as a direct representative for the families of the prisoners. Cheques were sent to the British Red Cross Society to cover the cost of food parcels for prisoners in Germany, and in July 1940 the director, the Right Honourable the Earl of Clarendon, wrote to Mrs German to assure her that money raised in this way would only be used for parcels for Leicestershire prisoners.

An indication of the variety of materials sent out to prisoners, and indeed the regularity with which they were received, comes once again from the diary of Leonard Bingley. On 16 December 1942 (which he describes as a lucky day) he records the arrival of a letter from his mother, two large parcels from the Lord Bishop of Leicester and even a gramophone from Mrs German. On 2 December 1943 he records a clothing parcel from Mrs German. The objective of the Leicestershire Prisoners of War Relief Committee was not merely to raise funds for POWs and to co-ordinate the sending of supplies to them (vital though this was). The organisation also acted as a source of welfare support to the families of those who were prisoners of war. On 4 February 1944 Private Joe White's mother wrote to him:

> I am waiting for the grand day to come to have you home again by my side, also see your sweet face once more. I keep praying every day for your return safely when the good old times come back ... The neighbours and all your work mates [are] asking me how you are going along. I am going to a Scouts concert at the Church Schools on Tuesday night. I belong to the Church Women's guild ... On Saturday I am going to a POW meeting [to hear] Mrs Guy German speak. Charlie & Lily are going with me. I have a magazine sent to me every month of the POW pictures for it is very nice reading letters of which you spend your time in various ways, so you can see I take a great interest in you my loved one Joe.[25]

With the coming of peace following VE Day, a welcome-home party was held for Leicestershire's returned prisoners of war. This took place at De Montfort Hall in Leicester on 23 June 1945. Present was General Sir Clive Liddell KCB CMG CBE DSO, the Colonel of the Leicestershire Regiment and his wife Lady Liddell, who was President of the Relatives Association. Warm tributes were paid to Mrs German, for her work for the Association over the previous five years. She was presented with bouquets of flowers on behalf of the officers, NCOs and men of the Leicestershire Regiment. Sir Clive's speech concluded with the words:

> Before I ask the President of the Relatives Association to welcome the return of the prisoners of war, I should just like to thank all the organisers, particularly Mrs Guy German, of the Leicestershire Prisoners of War Comforts Fund, and Post-War Care and Relatives Association, for the really excellent work they have carried out throughout the war.
>
> I am sure that the returned prisoners of war will have plenty to say in appreciation of the work carried out by this organisation and I think that it is a splendid thing to have formed this Relatives Association and hold these meetings where relatives can exchange news, talk to each other and help each other generally.[26]

Lady Liddell then gave a very warm welcome home to all the returned prisoners, and Mrs German herself responded by saying:

> It is my pleasure and honour to thank Sir Clive Liddell for so kindly coming to Leicester today to take the chair at our family reunion party.
>
> Sir Clive and Lady Liddell have always taken the greatest interest in our work and in the well-being of you all, and I know that it is your wish that that I should say on your behalf how happy we are to have them with us this afternoon.
>
> It seems almost too good to be true, to see so many families re-united. It has been my privilege to know many of you for a long time. We have had our ups and we have had our downs, but we have stood together in suffering and anxiety. We shall always remember with pride the high courage of our men and also remember with thankfulness that, under Providence, they came safely home from Germany. I hope that we may never forget our friendship and that whatever fate may hold in store we shall stand together.
>
> Our work for those who have been in Germany is nearly over, but our aim is not yet fully accomplished, for we have still nearly one thousand Leicestershire men in the Far East, and until they are home with their families we cannot feel that our work is finished. We hope we may do for them all that we have been able to do for you who have returned from Germany. I know that this is your wish and that we shall have failed if we cannot achieve it. Sir Clive and Lady Liddell are in entire agreement with this and will help and encourage our work until the war is truly over and we have a reunion party for the rest of the family who are at the moment so unhappily parted.
>
> I want you all to show your appreciation to Sir Clive and Lady Liddell for all they have done and are doing for our Association, and to say a very big 'Thank you'.[27]

Captain Sidney Brown spoke on behalf of the returned prisoners. He referred to the parcels the Association had sent out to them. He recalled many incidents of camp life in Germany, and remarked how useful the cigarettes contained within the parcels had been for bartering with Nazi guards for favours. He concluded: 'Mrs German's Christian name is Rosemary, which stands for remembrance. She never forgot us during those five years and we can assure her that not only have we not forgotten her but that we will always remember her.[28]

In the New Years Honours List published on 31 December 1946, Rosemary German was awarded the MBE for her work for the Leicestershire Prisoners of War Comforts Fund. It was a thoroughly deserved award, for unlike many of the other recipients whose names appeared in the *London Gazette* alongside hers, mainly men of industry and commerce who no doubt had made a healthy profit for themselves alongside producing armaments and munitions, her war work had truly made a difference to the lives of so many others. Indeed, it is no exaggeration to say that her efforts had probably saved the lives of many of the Leicestershire men in German prisoner of war camps. She was a remarkable woman.

Chapter 7

Aftermath

For many years, in the minds of the British people as a whole and for the men of the 2nd/5th Leicesters in particular, the events of the 1940 campaign were overshadowed by what came afterwards. With France out of the war by the end of June 1940, Britain stood alone against Hitler, devoid of allies beyond her own Empire and Commonwealth. The Battle of Britain, which followed hard on the heels of Dunkirk, saw the country pitched into a life or death struggle against the might of the Luftwaffe. Following directly on from this the Nazi high command tried a new tactic – the attempt to bomb Britain into submission by nightly attacks on towns and cities. To the Blitz, which lasted through the autumn and winter of 1940 and etched itself into the national memory, Dunkirk became just a prelude. The unsuccessful 1940 campaign, with its poverty of political and military leadership and the bitter division between Britain and France over what happened at Dunkirk, was also overshadowed by the sharply contrasting successful campaigns elsewhere, notably the British and American liberation of France and North West Europe in 1944–45.

For many of the men of the 2nd/5th Leicesters who had escaped from Dunkirk, this affair was only the prelude to a long and arduous series of campaigns which would see the battalion first rebuilt and then returned to active service. It absorbed the remnants of the 1st/5th battalion, which had faced a similarly harrowing experience in Norway, and then underwent an extensive training programme in England. It was 1942 before the battalion was ready to proceed overseas once more. Peter Moore was a newly commissioned officer who joined the battalion before it deployed overseas. He remembered:

> My platoon sergeant was Sergeant Grainger, a fine man, handsome in a rather gypsy way, and a veteran of Dunkirk. My other NCOs and soldiers had all served in France and I wondered how they would react to being commanded by a callow 21 year old who had seen no action, but I need not have worried. There was a wonderful esprit de corps in B company and in the whole battalion due, I am sure, to all of us being Leicestershire men apart from a few of the new draft.[1]

The revitalised 2nd/5th battalion landed in Tunisia as part of the British 1st Army, which was tasked with linking up with Montgomery's 8th Army. Men like 'Moe' Harper, Harold Simons and Gordon Spring would fight with the battalion through North Africa, on into Italy and would end the war in Austria. Along the way they faced some ferocious battles – Alf Nichols, having managed to avoid capture during the Dunkirk campaign, was taken prisoner by German forces at Kasserine Pass in Tunisia. During the Italian campaign, the battalion landed at Salerno and was involved in bitter fighting for the Gothic Line. Many of those men who had escaped via Dunkirk would leave their bones in Italian soil. Arthur Knight, who had survived the 1940 campaign in France and who had been evacuated at Dunkirk, was one of those who would lose his life in the fighting around Monte Cassino.

Yet the successful evacuation at Dunkirk was one of, if not the, key moment of the Second World War. The fact that the BEF was not destroyed in France, as might easily have happened, kept Britain in the war. It is no exaggeration to say that the fact that Britain fought on alone in 1940 probably saved democracy in Western Europe. The United States was still in the grip of neutrality; the Soviet Union was still in a non-aggression pact with the Nazis. Both would join the war later, but for now Britain (and her Empire and Commonwealth) fought the Germans alone. In the defeat of Hitler, Josef Stalin once commented that the United States had provided the money, the Soviet Union provided the blood, whilst Great Britain provided the time.

It is difficult to answer the question of which group of men suffered the hardest war after Dunkirk – those who had been taken prisoner or those who went on to fight with the battalion. This latter group at least had good rations and the occasional chance of leave, and were in reasonably regular contact with their families. If those in prisoner of war camps did not face the danger of combat on a regular basis they were nonetheless at the mercy of the German authorities on a day-in-day-out basis.

Almost all of those who served with the 2nd/5th in the Dunkirk campaign shared a degree of pride – justifiable pride – in what they had done and achieved. They had played a significant part in the defeat of Hitlerism, the most serious menace to British freedom and democracy of the twentieth century, and they had done so in what was a true 'citizen army'. The 2nd/5th battalion was the heir to the noble traditions of the Pals battalions of the First World War, when working men had stepped away from their lathes and come to their country's service in its hour of need. There was enormous pride too in having been part of the Leicestershire Regiment. If the battalion was diluted later in the war with recruits from all parts of the country, it should be remembered that in 1940 it was overwhelmingly recruited in the county. There was, and still is among survivors, a fierce local pride in having served in their county regiment.

The first reunion of the 1st/5th and 2nd/5th battalions was held at De Montfort Hall in Leicester on Saturday, 13 July 1946. It was attended by over 500 former members, some of them veterans of two world wars. Contingents came from all parts of the county, from Leicester and from Rutland. It was described in the press at the time as an astonishing gathering, with hundreds of men drinking beer and eating sandwiches in the warm summer evening air. The band of the Leicestershire Regiment played, and men who had not seen each other in some cases for five or six years shook hands once again. Senior officers present included Lieutenant Colonel Ruddle and Colonel Atkins, honorary colonel of the 2nd/5th battalion.

Men like Gordon Spring, Harold Simons and 'Moe' Harper are still attending annual reunions of the Royal Tigers Association seventy years after the events that first brought them together. Other ex-2nd/5th men became part of the Dunkirk Veterans Association. Alf Nichols, Kenneth Callaghan and no doubt others as well were members. Both Nichols and Callaghan remained so until their deaths in the 1990s. In the 1970s the Association, in conjunction with the town of Dunkirk, struck a commemorative medal for veterans, of which both men were holders. The medal was open to those who had been involved in the evacuation from Dunkirk in 1940 and to those who had been captured in the fighting that preceded it.

Some men returned embittered from their war experiences. Walter Graves, who had tried to intervene to save the life of the Russian prisoner, returned home in 1945 to a 6-year-old daughter he had never met. A fortnight after his return, his daughter had been playing in the street outside the family home in Leicester, where German prisoners of war were working relaying the road surface. One of the Germans had carved the little girl a toy dachshund from a piece of wood. When Graves found out where it had come from, he broke it in half and threw it on the fire.

Bob Monk, by contrast, carried no animosity towards the Germans after the war. He was aware that towards the end of the conflict the guards were suffering almost as much as the POWs. In fact, Monk often shared his cigarettes with his guards. Leonard Bingley similarly took a more charitable view of his German guards, telling his family many years later that the guards were often not much better off than their prisoners, and were often equally cold and hungry. His daughter remembers him being upset if any food was left at meal times, an understandable reaction to the starvation diet on the long march. Another daughter remembers as a child after the war having said, 'I'm starving', and being told that she was not starving, she was hungry, and there is a difference. His family recall that he did, in time, return to being the man they knew. Although Bingley had left a very ill son behind at home, which must have been an added strain during the years of captivity, it perhaps says something about him as a man that he held no bitterness towards the nation that kept him away from his young family for so long. He seemed to distinguish between the German war machine and the Germans as people, and was able to reason that the German soldiers also had families that they were away from. He was also a deep and spiritual man, but not in the orthodox way. Although he was by birth Church of England, he did not attend church, but had a deep faith and taught his children right from wrong and to be kind and thoughtful. His diary testifies to the fact that he turned to his faith to help him through the terrible time he undoubtedly went through emotionally during the war.

Maurice Jennings returned to his job in a grocery shop in Lutterworth, which had been kept open for him whilst he was in the Army. He believes that undoubtedly the experience of captivity changed him, as it did others. He harbours no bitterness now towards his German captors, believing that there is good and bad to be found in every nation. Likewise, Horace Greasley bore no malice towards the German people after the war; in retirement he counts Germans among some of his closest friends. The only grudge that he still carries is towards the British government, which he felt turned its back on the returning POWs after the war. Whilst other units were coming back to bunting and victory parades in 1945, the returning prisoners were largely ignored. This was in spite of the fact that the war would have been lost in 1940 were it not for these men, who had effectively sacrificed themselves to hold the Germans back from Dunkirk in order to allow others to be evacuated. To add insult to injury, he was owed nearly five years in back pay, from which the British government made a deduction for the food and lodgings that he had received in the prisoner of war camps! Horace sent his medals back to the War Office in disgust. Greasley is certain that his wartime experiences made him a stronger man, and in consequence of those experiences, he never worked for anyone else for the remainder of his working life. He was determined that after five years of being ordered about and shouted at, once back in Civvy Street that was never going to happen again. Thereafter, he always ran his own businesses and was his own boss.

Other men were also affected by the horrors that they had witnessed in the east. Philip Haywood's wife remembered that he would often sit quietly staring into the fire. He spoke little about what had happened in captivity, but he also remained adamant for the rest of his life that he would not be told what to do or when to do it by anyone again. Whilst the 'Dear John' letters, such as that received by Joe White, were almost an inevitable part of POW life, one doubts that the one that he received left a permanent scar. After all, such things also happened to young men in civilian life, and White married another woman soon after the war, but the sense of betrayal was perhaps compounded by his circumstances. It is not known how many marriages broke under the strain of enforced separation, but empirical evidence suggests the number must have been high. White also received news whilst he was a prisoner of the death of his mother at home in Leicester. More devastating was the news received by Company Sergeant Major Andrew Croxall whilst he was a prisoner of war, that his son Anthony had been killed fighting with the Leicestershire Regiment in North West Europe in 1944. It was said that he was never the same man again after this.

Other casualties of the campaign took a different form. Lieutenant Colonel Kenneth Ruddle was not a young man during the retreat to Dunkirk, and the strain of this most arduous campaign must undoubtedly have aggravated long-standing health problems. In 1942 Ruddle relinquished his commission in order to return to his brewery at Langham, and went on successfully to fight other battles. Twice in the years after the war, Rutland, under his leadership, fought off attempts by Westminster to amalgamate the tiny county with Leicestershire. He was chairman of Rutland County Council, an alderman, senior area chairman of the Conservative Party and was knighted for his services to Rutland in 1957. That same year, on 29 June, Ruddle represented the Royal Leicestershire Regiment at the unveiling by HM Queen Elizabeth The Queen Mother of the Dunkirk Memorial to the Missing, upon which the names of twenty of his men who were killed in the 1940 campaign, and whose bodies were not recovered, are recorded. Upon this sombre occasion he laid a wreath from the Colonel of the Regiment and all ranks. Sir Kenneth Ruddle died at Langham in September 1979.

Those who had stayed at home also suffered the after effects of the Dunkirk campaign. Cecil Botibol's parents divorced in the 1950s; their marriage did not survive the devastating impact of the loss of their only son. Freddie Diaper's parents were also traumatised by the loss of their son. His sister still remembers her surprise at seeing her father crying when he heard the news; as an 8-year-old girl she had never before seen a man crying. Freddie had only been married for six months, and his young widow Nellie remarried after the war, and raised a family. Corporal Andrew Quigley's widow never remarried. His son was born a few months after his death, and was named by his grieving mother in honour of the father he never knew, but of whom he is deeply proud.

The way each member of the 2nd/5th lived their lives after the war was as different as the men themselves. Harold Simons went back to the building trade which he had been in before the war. The industry was going through a boom as the post-war Labour government sought to redress the housing shortage that had been such a problem before the war, and which had been worsened by wartime bombing. He remembered that builders in those post-war years had to build five council houses before they were allowed to build one private house. Don French returned to the hosiery trade in which he had been before the war. Horace Greasley ran a taxi firm before emigrating to Spain in retirement in 1988. 'Moe' Harper worked for many years for Geoff Gee, his old company commander.

Sidney Brown returned to politics. He kept his seat on Leicester City Council and the high point of his political career came in 1958 when he served a term as Lord Mayor of Leicester. He remained interested in youth work and education throughout his life. He served on the Education Committee and Children's Committee of Leicester City Council, he served as chairman of governors of five secondary schools, including the one he had attended as a boy – Wyggeston School. He was awarded the Territorial Decoration after the war and remained in touch with his former regiment. In 1958, as Lord Mayor of Leicester, he represented the Corporation at the annual Royal Tigers Weekend and received a gift of a silver tiger as a token of appreciation of the goodwill that existed between the city and the regiment.

Ken Symington also remained with the Royal Leicestershire Regiment. After Dunkirk he had served on staff appointments in India and the Far East, but in 1947 he returned to take command of the reconstituted 5th battalion. In the immediate post-war years there was little interest or enthusiasm for service with the TA, but through his hard work and revival of regimental traditions he overcame these problems. In 1950 he handed over to his successor a fine and efficient battalion. He remained with the TA on staff appointments, acted as County Army Welfare Officer and became a Deputy Lieutenant of the county. He died in 1963, aged just 57. His obituary in the *Green Tiger* states: 'The early death of Kenneth has left a blank in the minds of all who knew him. Whenever and wherever he appeared he brought with him warmth and charm, a special grace and gentleness of manner ... He faced life as a "Great Adventure", courageously, gaily and always unselfishly ...[2]

Mike Moore went on to see much action in North Africa and Italy. After the war he returned to the family business of Moore Eady, where he became chairman and managing director. The firm then moved from Hinckley to Derby, where Mike is still remembered by former staff as a smart man in a pin-striped suit. He is also regarded as a kindly man who cared as much for the welfare of his workers as he did about profits. Mike also elected to stay on with the TA into the 1950s. He, like Ken Symington, eventually came to command the 5th battalion, before finally retiring from active soldiering in 1956. However, he would continue to serve his regiment, in one way or another, until his death in 1984. He was chairman of the Royal Tigers Association, and Deputy Honorary Colonel of the Royal Anglian Regiment.

Gordon Spring's mother put pressure on him to leave the Army in 1945, a decision he afterwards bitterly regretted. He wrote later:

> Thus I was turning my back on army life – what a mistake! I came out with a trade and a recommendation and memories some too bitter and cruel to erase from my mind, even today. It took me at least five years to settle back into things in England ... I got married in England but it was a failure ... as my story ends, I can say that by the grace of God I survived.[3]

In fact Gordon Spring seems to have quite clearly been suffering from what would today be diagnosed as post-traumatic stress disorder. His wartime memories sometimes cause him nightmares even today, and with a heart condition he has been advised by his GP not to discuss his experiences at great length, because of the stress this causes.

It might be argued that psychological trauma of one degree or another is really only to be expected among survivors who witnessed so much suffering, as the Dunkirk survivors did. Ian Noble experienced terrifying flashbacks in the last years of his life, while Joe White's daughter recalls a post-war coach holiday in Europe. Late at night, as the coach crossed the German border, guards came aboard to check passports and other formalities. White woke from his slumber to the sound of German voices. His daughter still recalls the look of terror on his face and the sweat on his brow, as for a few moments he believed he was still a prisoner. Bob Monk suffered nightmares for much of his life after the war. On one occasion, he awoke shouting in the middle of the night, grabbed an alarm clock in the belief that it was a grenade and tried to throw it through a window. In fact, Monk was affected in more ways than one by his experiences as a POW. Another legacy of his time as a German prisoner was that he had missed out on those critical years between about 17 and 23, when young men learn a trade. He had never completed his apprenticeship as a carpenter, and after the war he had no career to resume. For a time, he drifted from job to job. One of his first jobs was in a factory, but Monk hated being incarcerated in the building and could not last more than a few days before handing in his notice.

Captain John Marshall left the Leicestershire Regiment after Dunkirk in order to help raise Britain's fledgling Airborne forces, as did Sergeant Fred Smith, who went on to serve with the Parachute Regiment after it was formed in 1941. Marshall fought in North Africa with the 1st Airborne Division, before returning to the Leicestershire Regiment after the war. He served with the 1st Royal Leicesters in Korea, but his career was cut short by a terrible accident. Whilst on a family holiday to Ireland, he went into the sea to help his daughters who he believed were in difficulties. The daughters made it back to land safely but Marshall himself tragically drowned, as his wife looked on help-lessly from the shore. It was a bitter irony that Marshall should die under such circumstances after facing death so often during the war.

Richard Everard continued to serve with the 2nd/5th Leicestershire Regiment. A fellow officer recalls his unconventional character, but also his single-minded sense of purpose:

I first met Richard in 1942 when I was posted as a platoon commander a company of the 2nd/5th battalion of the Leicestershire Regiment in Kent, of which he was second in command. I discovered that he had an engaging touch of eccentricity. I remember particularly being told how, one night before my arrival, he had sent up a Golden Rain rocket. This was a spectacular multi-coloured rocket which was only to be used to signal a German invasion. Richard was on night patrol on Romney Marsh when I gathered he persuaded himself that German paratroopers had landed. Whatever the reason, he fired a Golden Rain rocket into the night sky and the whole of the army in South-East England stood to. Then he sur-rounded a signal box on the main railway line and ordered the astonished signalman, at gunpoint, to stop the London express so that he could search it for spies, which he did.[4]

Richard served through the Tunisian and Italian campaigns, until his war came to an end through injury when he stepped on a land mine in Italy. Geoff Gee, meanwhile, went on to fight in North Africa in 1942 and 1943, and later trained reinforcements. The pair remained lifelong friends, and godparents to one another's children. The bond that had been forged between them during the retreat to Dunkirk was immensely strong, and they presented one another with engraved tankards as reminders of those days in extremis. Richard Everard first began work on his memoir, *A Soldier's Tale*, in 1944. He revised it in 1951, again in 1954 and for the last time in 1968. He prefaced it with the following statement: 'I make no apology for this story because I feel that if we could recapture some of the spirit and comradeship of those years many of our present troubles and discontents would disappear.'[5] Richard Everard died in 1993.

In summing up, this book has been about that element which really interests most people who regard themselves as military historians. We realise that the men we study are not supermen, but ordinary people, faced with extraordinary circumstances. The way that they behaved in these circumstances is what fascinates us, for we ask ourselves how we would have behaved in such a situation. All of the men in this book faced situations that hopefully most of us who come after them will never have to face, and for that we owe them an immeasurable debt of gratitude.

Notes

Chapter 1

1. J. Ellison Platt, *Padre in Colditz*, London, 1978.
2. G. Spring, *Gordon the Tiger*, n.d.
3. The *Green Tiger*, August 1939, p. 100.
4. Ibid.
5. Ibid.
6. J. Kynoch, *The Naked Soldiers*, London, 1995, p. 1.
7. G. Arlott, tape-recorded interview.
8. R. Everard, *A Soldier's Tale*, unpublished memoir.
9. Ibid.
10. P. Moore, *No Need to Worry*, Bishop Wilton, 2000, p. 15.
11. The *Green Tiger*, November 1940, p. 239.
12. J.L. Harper, manuscript recollections.
13. D. French, tape-recorded interview.
14. Ibid.
15. Ibid.
16. Kynoch, *The Naked Soldiers*, p. 2.
17. L.F. Bingley, unpublished manuscript letter, 26 November 1939.
18. T. Lynch, 'Bayonets Against Tanks', in *Military Illustrated*, July 2009. A very comprehensive article covering the story of the 'digging divisions'.

Chapter 2

1. Everard, *A Soldier's Tale*.
2. Ibid.
3. The *Green Tiger*, August 1940, p. 230.
4. Spring, *Gordon the Tiger*.
5. Ibid.
6. V. Clough, tape-recorded interview.
7. Everard, *A Soldier's Tale*.

8. Ibid.
9. Ibid.
10. Ibid.
11. Ibid.
12. Ibid.
13. S. Brown, manuscript notes, 1941 (used by permission of the Record Office for Leicestershire, Leicester and Rutland).
14. Everard, *A Soldier's Tale*.
15. Ibid.
16. Brown, manuscript notes.
17. R. Sharp, manuscript notes, 1941 (used by permission of the Record Office for Leicestershire, Leicester and Rutland).
18. Clough, tape-recorded interview.

Chapter 3

1. Brown, manuscript notes.
2. Everard, *A Soldier's Tale*.
3. Harper, manuscript recollections.
4. Brown, manuscript notes.
5. Sharp, manuscript notes.
6. R. Vincent, letter to author.
7. Arlott, tape-recorded interview.
8. The *Green Tiger*, August 1940, p. 214.
9. Ibid.
10. M. Jennings, letter to author.
11. G.K.F. Ruddle, typescript report (used by permission of the Record Office for Leicestershire, Leicester and Rutland).
12. H. Greasley, correspondence with author.
13. French, tape-recorded interview.
14. Spring, *Gordon the Tiger*.
15. F. and J. Shaw, *We Remember Dunkirk*, Hinckley, 1990, p. 219.
16. Everard, *A Soldier's Tale*.
17. Ruddle, typescript report.
18. The *Green Tiger*, August 1940, p. 214.
19. Clough, tape-recorded interview.
20. The *Green Tiger*, August 1940, p. 215.
21. K. Noble, information submitted to BBC 'People's War' website: http://www.bbc.co.uk/ww2peopleswar/stories/83/a2310283.shtml.

22. Everard, *A Soldier's Tale*.
23. Ibid.
24. Ibid.
25. Spring, *Gordon the Tiger*.
26. G. Chaplin, statement made for MI9, 1945.
27. Ruddle, typescript report.
28. Shaw and Shaw, *We Remember Dunkirk*.
29. Clough, tape-recorded interview.
30. Spring, *Gordon the Tiger*.
31. Harper, manuscript recollections.
32. Ruddle, typescript report.

Chapter 4

1. Shaw and Shaw, *We Remember Dunkirk*, p. 83.
2. H. Simons, tape-recorded interview.
3. Ruddle, typescript report.
4. Shaw and Shaw, *We Remember Dunkirk*, p. 219.
5. Everard, *A Soldier's Tale*.
6. R. Collier, *Sands of Dunkirk*, London, 1961, p. 159.
7. Everard, *A Soldier's Tale*.
8. Ruddle, typescript report.
9. Spring, *Gordon the Tiger*.
10. K. Noble, information submitted to BBC 'People's War' website: http://www.bbc.co.uk/ww2peopleswar/stories/83/a2310283.shtml.
11. Collier, *Sands of Dunkirk*, p. 31.
12. Harper, manuscript recollections.
13. G.P. Nichols, letter to author.
14. Spring, *Gordon the Tiger*.
15. Clough, tape-recorded interview.

Chapter 5

1. French, tape-recorded interview.
2. Jennings, letter to author.
3. French, tape-recorded interview.
4. Ibid.
5. Ibid.
6. Ibid.

7. Arlott, tape-recorded interview.
8. Greasley, correspondence with author.
9. Arlott, tape-recorded interview.
10. R. Vincent, statement made for MI9, 1945.
11. A. Croxall, statement made for MI9, 1945.
12. Arlott, tape-recorded interview.
13. French, tape-recorded interview.
14. Ibid.
15. L. Bingley, manuscript diary, 1942–45.
16. Ibid.

Chapter 6

1. French, tape-recorded interview.
2. Ibid.
3. J.W.H. White, manuscript letter, 9 November 1941.
4. White, manuscript letter, 13 December 1942.
5. British Red Cross letter to J.W.H. White, 26 September 1942.
6. French, tape-recorded interview.
7. Ibid.
8. Ibid.
9. Arlott, tape-recorded interview.
10. Bingley, manuscript diary, 1942–45.
11. Ibid.
12. Chaplin, statement made for MI9, 1945.
13. H. Greasley, statement made for MI9, 1945.
14. Auschwitz Museum website (English version): http://en.auschwitz.org.pl.
15. R. Sharp, statement made for MI9, 1945.
16. Red Cross report, Oflag VIIB Eichstatt, November 1942.
17. Ibid.
18. Ibid.
19. Bingley, manuscript diary, 1942–45.
20. Ibid.
21. Greasley, correspondence with author.
22. French, tape-recorded interview.
23. Arlott, tape-recorded interview.
24. Bingley, manuscript diary, 1942–45.
25. K.C. White letter to J.W.H. White, 4 February 1944.

26. The *Green Tiger*, August 1945, p. 45.
27. Ibid.
28. Ibid.

Chapter 7

1. Moore, *No Need to Worry*, p. 15.
2. The *Green Tiger*, Autumn 1963, p. 120.
3. Spring, *Gordon the Tiger*.
4. Everard, *A Soldier's Tale*.
5. Ibid.

Bibliography

The following sources were used in the preparation of this book.

Published material

Collier, Richard, *The Sands of Dunkirk*, London, Collins, 1961. A valuable work including many first-hand accounts and anecdotes (including some by members of 2nd/5th Leicesters), only let down by its lack of an index.

Greasley, Horace, *Do The Birds Still Sing in Hell?*, Alicante, Libros International, 2008. An autobiographical novel based on the author's experiences with the 2nd/5th Leicesters in France and in captivity, including his extraordinary relationship with Rosa Rauchbach.

Kynoch, Joseph, *The Naked Soldiers*, London, Excalibur Press, 1995. A memoir mainly covering the author's experiences with the 1st/5th Leicesters in Norway. However, the author served initially with the 2nd/5th battalion.

Lynch, Tim, 'Bayonets Against Tanks', in *Military Illustrated*, July 2009. Superbly researched and illustrated account of the background and experiences of the Territorial 'digging divisions' sent to France in 1940.

Montefiore, Hugh Sebag, *Dunkirk – Fight to the Last Man*, London, Penguin 2006. An overview of the 1940 campaign by a respected modern historian.

Moore, Major Peter, *No Need To Worry*, Bishop Wilton, Wilton 65, 2000. An excellent memoir written by an officer who joined the battalion after Dunkirk, but nonetheless knew many of those who had been involved in the campaign.

Richardson, Matthew, *Fighting Tigers: Epic Actions of the Royal Leicestershire Regiment*, Barnsley, Pen & Sword, 2002. Contains a chapter on the 2nd/5th Leicesters in the Battle of France.

Shaw, Frank and Joan, *We Remember Dunkirk*, Hinckley, Echo Press, 1990. The Dunkirk evacuation described first-hand in the words of those who witnessed it. A valuable work covering the experiences of soldiers, sailors, nurses and civilians.

Spring, Gordon, *Gordon the Tiger*, n.d. Privately published memoir covering the author's military service. A worthwhile 'voice from the ranks' that counterbalances other sources mostly prepared by officers.

Thompson, General Julian, *Dunkirk – Retreat to Victory*, London, Sidgwick & Jackson, 2008. A weighty volume that provides a useful analysis of the campaign, by a former soldier. Looks at events at political and strategic level, but also contains a good account of the evacuation from the beaches.

Underhill, Brigadier W.E., *The History of the Royal Leicestershire Regiment*, Eastbourne, Anthony Rowe, 1957. Contains a chapter on the 2nd/5th Leicesters in France 1940. Much of the material in this history of the regiment was contributed by former or serving officers. The second part of the chapter was contributed by Richard Everard, and is almost identical to *A Soldier's Tale* referenced below. The first part, though not credited as such, is believed to have been written up from notes supplied by Major Kenneth Symington.

Various contributors, *Green Tiger*, various editions. The newspaper of the Royal Leicestershire Regiment. Contains contemporary reports on the doings of the 2nd/5th battalion. Also obituary notices.

Wilson, Patrick, *Dunkirk*, Barnsley, Pen & Sword, 2000, part of the Battleground Europe series. Although the 2nd/5th Leicesters are mentioned only briefly, this is a handy pocket guide to the 1940 campaign.

Unpublished material

At the National Archives, Kew:

WO166-4419 War Diary of 2nd/5th battalion Leicestershire Regiment, April–May 1940.

WO167-396 War Diary of 139th Brigade Headquarters, May–June 1940.

WO344 MI9 Ex-POW Debriefs. About 50 per cent of POWs appear to be represented. Those from the 2nd/5th Leicesters that were traced were:

Arlott, George	Greasley, Horace	Sharp, Robert
Chaplin, Gordon	Haywood, Philip	Vincent, Richard
Croxall, Andrew	Jennings, Maurice	White, David

At the Record Office for Leicestershire, Leicester and Rutland, Wigston, Leicester:

Leicester Evening Mail
Leicester Mercury

DE7221 Brown, Captain Sidney, manuscript notes on operations of HQ Company 2nd/5th Leicesters, May 1940 (prepared in captivity, written in an exercise book stamped 'Oflag VIB Gepruft').

DE7221 Ruddle, Lieutenant Colonel Kenneth, confidential report (covers events 25–29 May 1940).

DE7221 Sharp, Robert, manuscript notes on operations May 1940 (written in the same exercise book that was used by Brown, see above).

DE7221 Anonymous, notes on the activities of the 2nd/5th battalion The Leicestershire Regiment April/May 1940 (this document was clearly prepared by an officer, possibly Major Kenneth Symington. Similarities with Underhill's chapter referred to above suggest that he was aware of it. The final entry is for 25 May 1940).

Privately held material

Bingley, Leonard, manuscript letter and diaries, 1939–45.

Clough, Victor, tape-recorded interview.

Everard, Richard, *A Soldier's Tale*, unpublished memoir.

French, Don, tape-recorded interview.

Harper, J.L., manuscript recollections.

Simons, Harold, tape-recorded interview.

White, Joe, manuscript letters and postcards, 1940–45.

Web sources

(All URL details correct at time of publication.)

http://www.bbc.co.uk/ww2peopleswar – online resource containing memories of wartime experiences, submitted to the BBC by members of the public.

http://www.wartimememories.co.uk/ – similar online resource to above, but privately run.

http://www.wwiimemories.com/ – another similar private online venture.

http://en.auschwitz.org.pl – official website of the Auschwitz Museum.

http://www.pegasusarchive.org – online resource containing much material concerning British POWs in the Second World War.

Index